Buffalo Bill, Boozers, Brothels, and Bare-Knuckle Brawlers

Buffalo Bill, Boozers, Brothels, and Bare-Knuckle Brawlers

An Englishman's Journal of Adventure in America

Kellen Cutsforth

TWODOT®

GUILFORD, CONNECTICUT
HELENA, MONTANA

A · T W O D O T® · B O O K

An imprint and registered trademark of Rowman & Littlefield

Distributed by NATIONAL BOOK NETWORK

British Library Cataloguing-in-Publication Information available

Library of Congress Cataloging-in-Publication Data

Booth, Evelyn, 1860-1901.
  Buffalo Bill, boozers, brothels, and bare-knuckle brawlers : an Englishman's journal of adventure in America / [transcribed and edited by] Kellen Cutsforth.
    pages cm
  Includes bibliographical references and index.
  ISBN 978-1-4422-4659-1 (hardback : alkaline paper)—ISBN 978-1-4422-4660-7 (ebook)
  1. Booth, Evelyn, 1860-1901—Diaries. 2. British—United States—Diaries. 3. Adventure and adventurers—United States—Diaries. 4. Booth, Evelyn, 1860-1901—Travel—United States. 5. Booth, Evelyn, 1860-1901—Friends and associates. 6. Buffalo Bill, 1846-1917. 7. United States—Description and travel. 8. Outdoor life—United States—History—19th century. 9. Nightlife—United States--History—19th century. 10. United States—Social life and customs—1865-1918. I. Cutsforth, Kellen. II. Title.
  E168.B74 2015
  973.8--dc23
                                2015014641

∞™ The paper used in this publication meets the minimum requirements of American National Standard for Information Sciences—Permanence of Paper for Printed Library Materials, ANSI/NISO Z39.48-1992.

CONTENTS

Foreword

BY STEVE FRIESEN

At a time when their less adventurous friends were embarking on safe but clichéd grand tours of the European capitals, a group of young friends took a "buddy trip" from England to America. While there they would carouse through several states, meet one of the most famous celebrities of their day, and experience a journey that was probably the most memorable of their lives. Among the young men was Evelyn Booth, who acted as scribe for the group, recording their experiences in a blue leather diary. The trip account was not, however, confined to his voice alone. One of his friends, John Percival Frizzle, interjects occasional sections and thoughts as well. Editor and author Kellen Cutsforth provides copious endnotes, providing a back story for the diary. The creation of these collaborators, including Cutsforth, is an entertaining, often ribald, and informative guide to the intrepid group's adventures in the New World.

 The journey began in fall of 1884 with an act of petty larceny, the pilfering of a crate of ducks that were later distributed at a London pub (later in his journey, and thousands of miles away, he learns a warrant has been issued for his arrest). After this last bit of mischief before their trip, Booth and companions head to Liverpool and depart for the States the next day. As the fellows head off on their journey so does the reader. Within the first few pages, it is clear that the reader's journey through the book will be greatly enhanced by Booth's wit and unveiled frankness. Not a mere recounting of facts, the Booth document offers a combination of travelogue and social commentary. The first order of the day for the travelers—food and drink. Booth pronounced the dessert at dinner as a year old and records "Beer bad and whisky good on this vessel." From the beginning Booth introduces the reader to the slang of the day, noting that the ship is occupied by a great many "Gougers." This is helpfully translated by Cutsforth as referring to extremely aggressive males. Those were not to be the last Gougers they would meet.

The comrades arrived in New York City and immediately compiled a list of gaming houses and houses of prostitution that must be visited. Over the next several weeks, they took advantage of these establishments, in addition to attending prize fights and drinking rather copious amounts, as they caroused their way through the city.

Finally acknowledging that a continued stay in New York City will be bad not only for their pocketbooks but their health, the group headed west with Denver as their objective. They actually did some sightseeing at Niagara Falls, where Booth made some observations about the falls and their environs. He declared that they were somewhat disappointing, due primarily to the commercialism. The group couldn't help but notice a dead horse floating in a whirlpool; they resolved to come back the next day and use it for target practice.

One of the companions' primary objectives, in addition to carousing, was hunting. While in Chicago they heard that there was plenty of game to be found in "Arkansaw" and modified their plans, heading south for most of December. After some time spent hunting in Texas, the companions traveled to New Orleans, where they visited Buffalo Bill's Wild West several times. Booth observed, "I fear the "'Hon. Cody'" is having a bad time of it, as there are hardly any spectators and his expenses must be very heavy."

Booth saw Buffalo Bill's Wild West at the beginning of what turned out to be, as Booth observed, a disastrous winter season. He had completed two summer seasons since beginning the Wild West in 1883 and decided he could continue the show through the winter if he took it to a warmer clime. He chose New Orleans, which was also hosting the World's Industrial and Cotton Centennial Exposition. Perhaps he thought the world would beat a path to the city for the Exposition. Things did not go well. The trouble began when the riverboat transporting the show down the Mississippi crashed and sank, taking most of the sets to the bottom of the river and killing a lot of the livestock. Fortunately none of the performers were hurt. Cody and his partner postponed their New Orleans opening by two weeks and were able to get the Wild West back together in time to open just before Christmas. But rainy weather, a streetcar strike, and overall poor attendance at the exposition made the New Orleans engagement a losing proposition. When the show closed in April, they had accumulated $60,000 in debts. Cody almost closed his show for good during the stay in New Orleans but soldiered on to fame and fortune.

Booth and friends' experience in New Orleans was not any better than Cody's. The weather was miserable and they had several run-ins with the law. He noted, "Thank goodness our remittances have arrived from New York and we can leave this horrid place." With money from home in hand, the comrades headed farther south to Florida. There they continued to have a variety of adventures and misadventures, including a great deal of hunting, fishing, and even a strange encounter with a corpse.

The names Buffalo Bill and Cody were used several times in somewhat strange contexts by Booth in his journal, probably in reference to persons using those nicknames. For example, on March 12, 1885, the traveling companions left an acquaintance, who Booth referred to as the Hon. Cody, in bed in Florida and returned to Louisiana. As Cutsforth points out in his notes, that particular acquaintance could not have been Buffalo Bill Cody, who was not in Florida but was still performing in New Orleans. The choice of "Buffalo Bill" as a nickname was not unusual. As early as March 20, 1874, Colorado's Las Animas Leader reported that "Buffalo Bill was killed again at Fort Scott last Monday, and now we have only seven more."

In New Orleans Booth was finally formally introduced to the actual Buffalo Bill. The introduction led to a shooting match between Booth and Buffalo Bill, which Booth wins by three. Buffalo Bill requested a rematch the following week, which he won. In the intervening days Booth and his friends hung out with the cowboys from Buffalo Bill's Wild West, including Buck Taylor. This section of the journal provides valuable insight into how Wild West performers spent their time off as well as providing other details concerning the show.

Buffalo Bill's friendship with Booth while in New Orleans turned out to be a stroke of good fortune during that disastrous winter season. Later, in 1886, he needed an infusion of cash and Booth was able to help out his newfound friend with a loan of $30,000. In New Orleans Buffalo Bill was considering taking the show to England and discussed it with Booth. Those conversations helped set Cody on the course of taking his show to Europe. That finally happened in 1887 when Buffalo Bill's Wild West was invited to appear in London at the Golden Jubilee celebration of Queen Victoria's reign.

Kellen Cutsforth has done a real service by discovering, editing, and bringing forth the Booth diary. Booth is very frank about subjects that were taboo in polite society of the time, and continue to be so today. And the camaraderie of the travelers is dealt with forthrightly, from cavorting in bordellos to dealing with each other's hangovers. One is tempted to dwell upon the revelations of the bawdier side of the Gilded Age, sanding some of the gilt away. But beyond appealing to prurient curiosity in several places, there are descriptions of places, people, and circumstances that should be of use to any observer of the past. The diary is filled with interesting first-hand information about the era, ranging from a recounting of foods and drinks popular at the time to observations about the conveniences and inconveniences of travel. And the information shared about Buffalo Bill and his Wild West performers during the early years of the show is invaluable. If I have any disappointment with the diary, it is that the group never made it to Denver as originally intended. I'm sure they would have provided some interesting observations about my hometown.

INTRODUCTION

Evelyn Booth's journal begins October 24, 1884, and concludes April 1885. It is an important contribution to the history of America's Gilded Age during the latter half of the nineteenth century. The journal is housed in the Denver Public Library's Western History and Genealogy Department.

Born in 1860 to well-to-do English parents in Dublin, Ireland, Evelyn Thomas Barton Booth attended Trinity College in Cambridge, England.[1] Two years after his graduation, he and two wealthy companions, Reginald Beaumont Heygate and Dr. John Percival Frizzle, ventured to the States to sample all that the burgeoning country had to offer.[2] They would eventually be joined by the most famous horse jockey of the day, Englishman Frederick James Archer.

America's Gilded Age had brought on an opulent self-indulgence prevalent throughout the American upper class, and eventually spawned the world's modern industrial economy. The industrialized nation's "super rich" and economic elite reshaped and reenvisioned a country that was maturing and beginning to realize its true potential as an industrial power. Accompanying this new found wealth was a freshly discovered sense of openness and adventure that many well-to-do travelers, like Evelyn Booth, were all too eager to experience.

American popular culture was beginning to seep into all the crevices of society as well. Former buffalo hunter, Indian fighter, and civilian scout Colonel William Frederick "Buffalo Bill" Cody was beginning to realize the potential of his Wild West show. This entertainment spectacle would soon come to define and forever shape the idea of the "Wild West" in the hearts and minds of the American public. The American love of sport also began to grow at a fever pitch. Heavyweight pugilist John L. Sullivan was the most famous and renowned American of the day. He ruled the boxing ring with size and power, destroying opponents with shear brute force. Sports like baseball and horse racing were reaching new heights of popularity as well. Heroes, worthy of the title or not, were being forged and a country was being built. There was nothing to stop it from surging into the twentieth century.

As these young sportsmen traveled from New York to Chicago to Arkansas and finally to New Orleans, they caroused in infamous brothels, frequented gambling houses, and obtained front row seats at a John L. Sullivan heavyweight boxing title fight. But their greatest adventure came while in New Orleans. Booth eventually struck up a friendship with the famous showman Buffalo Bill Cody, who was performing there with his Wild West show.[3] The newfound friendship eventually led to two highly publicized target-shooting contests between the men.[4] There is some question, however, as to when Booth and Buffalo Bill Cody first became acquainted. The two definitely knew each other in New Orleans and eventually had business dealings with each other afterward, but Booth and his companions had a propensity for using nicknames and may have used the nickname "Buffalo Bill" for someone they met while on the hunting trail in Arkansas. Whatever the case, Booth and Cody eventually became fast friends and entered into a lucrative partnership.

After recording his adventures in this journal, Booth returned to England but he would not remain there long. In 1886, Booth would again venture to the United States.[5] While there, he entered into a lucrative contract with Buffalo Bill, helping him to find firm financial footing after experiencing many fiscal follies.[6] The contract allowed Booth to receive 25 percent of the profits the Wild West show made for three years.[7] Booth also helped Cody hatch the idea of taking the Wild West overseas to England, which transformed the enterprise into an international phenomenon. After their agreement ended, it seems that Booth and Cody did not continue their friendship. Evelyn Booth, however, remained in the United States where he would continue to live the sporting man's life wagering heavily on boxing fights and horse races and would also own some ranchland in Wyoming.[8] After a brief stint in Canada's Klondike, with his wife Lola, Booth settled in Oregon. In August 1901, Booth died at the age of forty-one from burns he received in a brush fire.[9]

Unlike Booth, Reginald Beaumont Heygate would go on to live a rather uneventful life. Born in 1857 in London, England, to Constance

M. and William Unwin Heygate, a magistrate for the county of Hertfordshire, England, Reginald graduated from Cambridge University with a B.A. in 1880 and an M.A. in 1883. He eventually found work as an assistant private secretary to Sir William Harcourt in 1886 but died unmarried in 1903.[10]

Dr. John Percival Frizzle was born in Belfast, Ireland, in 1862. Frizzle, after returning to the United Kingdom in 1885, would eventually emigrate to the United States in 1889. He married Sarah Sadie W. Rhodes in 1894. After the marriage ended, Frizzle remarried in 1905 to Lena Frances Parker. The couple had twin girls, Lena Parker Frizzle and Frances Percival Frizzle. The family lived in Northern California, in Siskiyou County.[11] Like Evelyn Booth, Frizzle spent time in British Columbia's Klondike and Yukon Territory. Later in life, Dr. Frizzle would gain some notoriety for organizing an attempt to track a mastodon he believed was living in the Alaskan wilderness.[12]

Horse jockey Frederick James Archer was one of the most famous and renowned Englishmen of the day. Born in 1857, Archer became a champion horse jockey by the age of fifteen and quickly rose to prominence becoming England's most celebrated horseman during the late nineteenth century. During his short but storied career, Archer won the Epsom Derby five times and won twenty-one other classic races.[13] A close friend of Evelyn Booth's, Archer arrived in America in December 1884.[14] He quickly joined Booth and his companions while they caroused throughout the country. Although he seemed to have everything, Archer committed suicide only a short time later in 1886. It is reported that his death, from a self-inflicted gunshot wound, was brought on by massive weight loss stemming from his constant binge dieting to maintain his weight as a jockey, a bout with a fever, and severe depression from the loss of his wife, Nellie Rose Dawson, who died in 1884.[15]

Booth's narrative, highlighted with rough-hewn humor and biting wit, examines the American fascination with sport with descriptions of boxing, horse racing, baseball, gambling, and hunting and fishing game all over the country. Booth also provides a European viewpoint of this emerging America and seamlessly combines the sporting life and extraordinary adventure into one volume.

EDITOR'S NOTE

The 1884–1885 travel journal is a blue leather bound diary 13 x 8¼ inches with legal size pages and the words "1885 Diary" on the cover. This folio diary was produced by "T. J. and J. Smith's Ready Reference" and contains an almanac. The pages have yellowed and loosened over time but are in good condition. Many of the illustrations and photographs reproduced in this volume were either pasted inside the journal's pages or placed in them loosely.

The journal was purchased in 1975 by the Denver Public Library. The journal is 381 pages in length. Pages 7–8 and 23–24 are missing. Pages 94–99, 102–112, 116–365, and 368–372 are blank.

The journal is well written and was not difficult to read except for an occasional misspelling. Booth, when describing his companions, would often refer to them by their initials: Fred Archer became FA, Reginald Heygate became RH or R, and John Percival Frizzle became F. In order to clarify which companions Booth was writing about, I spelled out their names. The journal, in a few sections, is written by two separate people; Evelyn Booth and J. P. Frizzle. Booth authors the majority of the text while J. P. Frizzle often adds a corroboration of events or his thoughts on a subject. To ease the transition of authors for the reader, I have identified who is writing the passages by placing the author's name in italics and within brackets.

I believe that most of the journal's narrative was written a few days after the events Booth describes took place. The journal has been transcribed as accurately as possible. There is lack of punctuation and paragraph breaks throughout the journal so a literary transcription style was used to create paragraph breaks and to add punctuation and capitalization where obvious. The author's spelling and grammar was not altered. I have, however, added words to sentences in brackets to help with the ease of reading.

Parentheses, dashes, underlining, and abbreviations are Booth's own unless otherwise noted. There is very little use of [sic] throughout, but it was added in portions of the narrative deemed necessary to clarify the text. Illegible words are indicated by [_____]. The section titled "Points on America," found in the conclusion of chapter 6, was moved from its original position in the journal. I moved the section, written by Booth before he boarded the steamship "Floridian," to the conclusion of chapter 6 to provide finality to the narrative.

All items found within the journals pages have been reproduced as images or transcribed in the appendix. The only items not reproduced in this volume are a piece of letterhead from Chicago's Palmer House Hotel and a doodle found on page 373.

ACKNOWLEDGMENTS

Thanks to Dr. Jefferson Broome whose encouragement and guidance have helped me through years of research; to Steve Friesen whose mutual interests, professionalism, and personal research were a great help to me; to Ann Brown for helping to discover this journal; to Dennis Hagen for being a great friend, for informative conversations, and guiding me along the way; to Ellen Zazzarino for her encouragement and direction; to Jim Kroll and Abby Hoverstock for allowing me to publish this unique journal; to Chris Enss for giving me the opportunity to get this work noticed; and to Erin Turner for her editorial insight. And to artist Tyrell Cannon for his brilliant illustrations that highlight this book. I am also indebted to my beautiful and loving wife Meghan and amazing daughter Cora who have supported me through years of work and research.

I am grateful to the following institutions, individuals, and agencies that helped locate and provided important manuscripts, documents, and photographs: the entire staff at the Western History and Genealogy Department at the Denver Public Library; Buffalo Bill Center of the West; Buffalo Bill Grave and Museum; History Colorado; Library of Congress; and the New Orleans Public Library.

CHAPTER ONE

The Journey to America

[This list is the itinerary of the day written by Evelyn Booth.]
Friday
October 24th, 1884
England

10 a.m. – The Grove [_____]
12.30. – New Market
5.30. – Shots
6.0. – Br
6.30. – Stole crate of ducks
7.0. – Station
7.30. – Throw out a three carder
8.30. – Invasion of bar at St. Pancras[1] by man, ducks
8.35. – Capture and with drawl of many ducks
9.0. – Criterion
10.0. – Distribution of ducks
12.0 – Leave for Liverpool[2]

Cunard Steamship S.S. *Oregon*[3]
Saturday
October 25, 1884
We left Liverpool at 8 minutes to 2 after thoroughly inspecting the vessel and "visiting" the immigrants who are principally Norish.[4] Having rolled into the doctor's room by mistake we immediately struck up "ditto the purser."[5] The first result of the afore said friendship is an assault on Regy's[6]

A Cunard Line steamship, the *Oregon* began operation in 1884 and would later sink in 1886. LIBRARY OF CONGRESS

wine case, which succumbs to repeated well directed pricks on the part of Frizzle.[7]

Good old Brown and Bingham Jack[8] having departed blind and paralytic[9] some time previous. Never before were such a cruel lot of gougers[10] seen together as on this vessel. The only celebrities appear to be Adelina Patti[11] (looking the worse for wear), Greenfield,[12] the pug, and two members of the Salvation Army[13] in full uniform. Both of these gentlemen's hair is in great need of a visit from the barber and several have been heard to say that their helmets will be missing before Sandy Hook is reached.

The first meal produced a fair muster evidently meaning to lay in provision for the voyage table, [the meal was] very fair except [for] dessert, which was a year old (nuts particularly) Beer bad and whisky good on this vessel. Yanks do not show to advantage on these occasions and their dress too much resembles that of a mute to invite a closer acquaintance. [I] have discovered a sportsman in the person of the smoke room waiter. He even backed Florence for a place and knows a "certainty" for the Liverpool Cup.[14]

Adelina Patti (1843–1919) was one of the most well-known and world-renowned opera singers of the 19th Century. LIBRARY OF CONGRESS

Say, Heard on S.S. "*Oregon*": Waiter, "What Will you take Miss?" Fair Yank, "I guess I'd take Venice but I ain't through yet."

[The following entry is written by John Frizzle.]
Arrived in Queenstown[15] all right [at] 7.30 a.m. [I] had a very good breakfast, inspected ship and emigrants. Went on shore [at] 12.30 [and] met Cronyn [sic] and went for "Coffey" to Queens Hotel.[16] Walked about Queenstown till it was time to go back to "*Oregon*" [and I] bought [a] blackthorn stick and Bogwood[17] pipe from a Queenstown tart.

Heygate arrived with the "Beril" [which was] good by tram and Dublin.[18] 3 o'clock p.m. finds us on board the "*Oregon*" once more. We are off. (Drink the order of day.) [There was] nothing else particular till dinner time. Five o'clock came. We three turn down for the "batch"[19] which is done justice too. The ship gives us the first lurch [and] turning to Heygate I said, "Did you feel that?" "I did," he said. "It's gone."

[I] retired to the smoking room [where] we began on Rye Whiskey which was very good indeed. Greenfield is in our party (Prize Fighter). He, after getting the taste of rye whisky, departed for the night. I got into [a] society with a yank and tossed him in (5 for 5) [and I] won a fiver in a few minutes. [I] made a match for St. [_____] too run of his two miles for $50,000 dollars. [I] am afraid that it will not come off.

Ships run 240 miles.

[The following entry is written by Evelyn Booth.]
Greenfield and Frizzle [were] standing outside [the] smoke room on [the] main deck [and] both [were] very strong. Says one, "This is only a big duck pond." [The] *Oregon* [then] ships a sea and soaks them both and they disappear.

Say: "It's lovely on deck Heygate!" "Why the hell don't you stay there!" answers Reginald with his head under the bed clothes.

[I went] down in [to] the saloon at 10 p.m. giving [the] waiters the cart wheel they opened their eyes at us in great style. One waiter who got the name "Paddy Maloney" gave out the "say."

Say: "I guess he's a whole team and a horse extra."

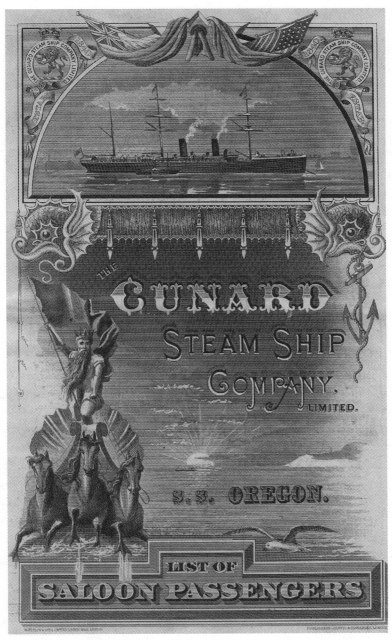

First Class Saloon Passenger List for S.S. *Oregon* DENVER PUBLIC LIBRARY

[The following entry is written by John Frizzle.]
Monday
27th 84
S.S. *Oregon*
(Got through the night), (All well). [I] had breakfast at 9 o'clock a.m. very rough. Everyone [is] sick but our noble sailors. Went and had a shave and came on deck. Heygate [was] in bed all day. I am going for lunch. [I] went and had a good one. Saw Salvation "Dangle Berry's" looking very bad; [with] No one about, [I went] down to see Heygate, he told me he had delivered up a few biscuits and a little "bile."[20] [I] made great friends with [an] emigrant girl, but find she is married after all so no "fit" to be had. [There is] nothing particular till before dinner when the Chief Steward got [a] fractured femur.

5 o'clock dinner time did not take batch so well but "Beril" [was] good. Old father[21] very bad looked for all the world as if he had "gonorrhea."

Ships run 352 miles.

Tuesday
28th Oct. 84
S.S. *Oregon*
Up at 7.30 a.m. [I] went and had a good wash. Very fine morning [I] walked about [the] deck till breakfast time [and] saw our old yank who we had a fight with [and] he looked very bad indeed. 8 o'clock, gong sounded [and I] went for the batch and had a very good one. Saw our friend Maloney from "Bruff."[22] He said he would get Salvation Army caps all night before the vessel got to New York. After breakfast, [I] came up on deck and sat down beside [a] very fine girl but it was no go. [I] got into [a] conversation with American "stick in the mud" [and] he asked me to go see him at his residence when we got over, [he] gave me his name (Mr. Kaskel).[23]

Heygate [was] much better [at] 1 o'clock [for] lunch time. [I] went and had a very good one after that [I] went and had a cigar and [was] on the deck again. Heygate brought his sooner for a walk and it left its "card"[24] about the vessel in great style. [I] had another go for [a] fair yank no go yet; better luck another time.

Had [a] great talk with [the] emigrants one of the girls [is] rather good looking [and I] brought her some ginger.[25] [I'm] thinking to get short time. "No go." [There was] nothing particular till 5 o'clock p.m. Dinner came, once more good "Beril," Heygate [was] down. Also, [there was a] very fat "father" behind me eating everything [and] at the same time [a] good lot of H2S[26] about him. [I] hope to see him no more. Heygate just came in with news that he got introduction to very nice girls, gives out that he is a man again. Old yanks name [is] Campell.

Ships run 390 Miles.

Wednesday
29th 84
S.S. *Oregon*
Up at 7 o'clock went on deck and bought chains. Walked about till breakfast time. Very fine morning [I] saw Miss Clinton and went and sat with her on deck [it] came on very rough about lunch time, never saw it so bad.[27] [There was] nothing particular, seemed very poor show at dinner, by this time [it was] very rough. In smoking room after dinner, fellow looks very inebriated. Pool [is] going on, and cards as usual. Saw Old Campbell he's going on about his shooting and fishing in Yankey [sic] land in great style.

Thursday
October 30th, 84
S.S. *Oregon*
Very fine morning but at 12 o'clock, [it] turned out [to be] very rough and wet up on deck for some time. Heygate and his girl [are] there, "the former on the right road to flash it," Evelyn Booth played cards with [a] Parson and made [an] example of him. Saw Greenfield [and] gave him some Glycerin and [_____] O'Conner[28], Heygate, Evelyn Booth and myself turned into [the] cabin at 12 o'clock to drink Anaconda Brandy.[29] Heygate and O'Connor [are] getting very "full."[30] I went to talk to Miss Clinton and [her] companion and returned at 3 o'clock to find Heygate very full indeed. As for O'Connor he was "blind."

5 o'clock dinner time all three [of us] meet once more. Heygate [is] doing nothing but laugh after supper went to see my girl [and] had [a] great

Portrait of Evelyn Booth (1860–1901) DENVER PUBLIC LIBRARY

talk with her. 7 o'clock comes, [and] our worthy friend Reginald Heygate returns from [the] upper deck very drunk [and] gives out that he was singing songs with the sailors and drinking brandy also. O'Connor [is] with him; don't know which was the most intoxicated. I unfortunately introduced him to my girl. He, Heygate, talks of nothing but her "bush." She, Miss Clinton, informs him that he is a little "Fresh." They remove themselves to [the] smoking saloon. See Heygate again at 10 o'clock in bed [and] think as I look at him there that the stomach pump would be advisable, [looks] nothing short of alcoholic poisoning. [I] Met [a] very nice fellow [by] the name of Richardson[31] from Colorado he gives [me] wonderful information about the country.

[The following statements are jokes being told by passengers, recorded by Evelyn Booth.]
Old Father to yank, "What sort is that melon?"
Mrs. Phipps,[32] "Is it ripe? Guess!?!"
Father, "It is ripe."
Josiah – Why won't you marry me Rebecca?
Rebecca – Because we have not one point in common.
Josiah – Suppose we was traveling and came to a house where there was only two beds and there was a man in one and a woman in the other. Which one would you get into?
Rebecca – The woman's of course.
Josiah – Well I reckon we have one point in common!!!
Ships run 434 miles

Oct. 25 – Left Liverpool 2 p.m.
Oct. 26 – 240 miles – Arrived at Queenstown
Oct. 27 – 352 miles – 7.30 left 4 p.m.
Oct. 28 – 390 miles – Strong Breeze
Oct. 29 – 434 miles – ditto
Oct. 30 – 314 miles – Heavy Sea
Oct. 31 – 422 miles – Very Fine
Nov. 1 – 467 miles – Rolling Very Much
Nov. 2 – 421 miles – Sandy Hook
[On November 2, 1884, the S. S. Oregon *docked in Sandy Hook, New Jersey.]*

CHAPTER TWO

The Falls, Fights, and Big City Nights

[At this point, the travelers have arrived in New York City. The following is a list of names and addresses of known gamblers, brothels, and sporting establishments compiled by Evelyn Booth.]

Saturday
Nov. 8th, 84
Hoffman House[1]
(Schedule)
"00" at New York
Mr. John Daily[2]
39 W 29[3]
Single O[4]
Mr. Read[5]
5 W 24[6]
Double O
Gus Abel [sic][7]
818 B.wy[8]
Champion at the [_____]
Faro at Chicago
Quick Gunn [sic][9]
124 Clark and 98 Randolph St.[10]
Hankins[11]
125 Clark Street
Hynes[12]
119 Clark Street[13]

Do at New Orleans
C. Bush[14]
32 Charles Street[15]
18 Royal Street[16]
(Keno do)
12 Royal
Budd Renaux [sic][17]
4 Royal

[The following entry is written by John Frizzle.]
Saturday
Nov. 8th, 84
Hoffman House
Weather charming; get up early and have some breakfast [and] go for a short walk afterwards. Mrs. Burgess[18] arrives [and] I find her in the drawing room we sit there for some time. She goes and is to be back at 1.30 for lunch. I go into Madison Square and smoke a cigar the hour arrives and [I] meet Heygate at [the] shop, next [I went to] Hoffman House, Mrs. Burgess appears go and have lunch with her. Heygate and Evelyn come and sit right opposite. They give out the "crack"[19] in great style. After lunch, walk down Broadway [and] go to see Eden Musee in (55 West 23rd Street).[20] Go and have strawberry ice in winter garden[21] and [a] bottle of wine. Go home with Mrs. Burgess afterwards and have tea. Introduced to fine fowls, one in particular [is] a very hot one. Mrs. Burgy wants stuffing badly. J.P.F.[22]

[The following entry is written by Evelyn Booth.]
Sunday
9th November 84
Hoffman House
Very fine morning awake and find my bed in a wreck after Reginald's encounter during the night. The sides and bottom [are] completely gone, [my] room [is] in a frightful state get up and have [a] bath. In the evening, go round to Mr. Barretts[23] and have encounter with "officer" outside. The latter does not get the best of it. Lie in bed all day and take Jamaica Ginger and endeavor to get "Mamie" but am failed by the woman.

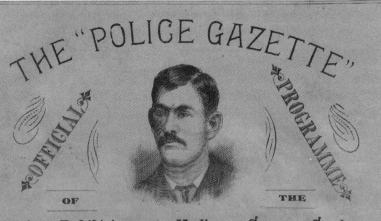

THE "POLICE GAZETTE"

OFFICIAL · PROGRAMME

OF · THE

Boxing ∴ Exhibition ∴ at ∴ Madison ∴ Square ∴ Garden !

MONDAY EVENING, NOVEMBER 10, 1884,

——BETWEEN——

JOHN L. SULLIVAN ← & → PROF. JOHN H. LAFLIN.

The Champion of Champions.   The Champion Athlete.

PATRICK SHEEDY, of Chicago,   BILLY MAHONEY, of Boston,
MANAGER.   **MASTER OF CEREMONIES.**

⁕ PROGRAMME ⁕

COMMENCE AT 8.30 P. M.

FIDDLER NEARY,   and   **JACK KEENAN,**
OF NEW YORK.   OF PHILADELPHIA.

8.45 P. M.

JOE FOWLER,   and   **GEORGE YOUNG.**
Feather-weight Champion of England.

9.00 P. M.

TOM ALLEN   and   **JIMMY KELLY.**

9.15 P. M.

JACK DEMPSEY,   and   **TOM FERGUSON,**
Champion Light-weight Pugilist of America.   OF PHILADELPHIA.

10.00 P. M.

JOHN L. SULLIVAN,   AND   PROF. JOHN H. LAFLIN.
The Champion of the World.

⋟ PRICE 10 CENTS ⋞

John L. Sullivan vs. John Laflin fight program DENVER PUBLIC LIBRARY

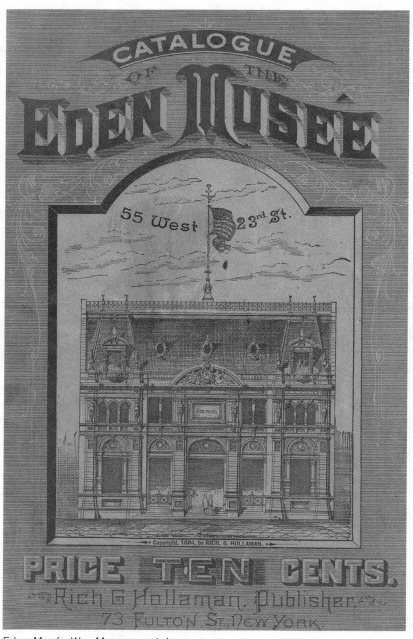

Eden Musée Wax Museum catalogue DENVER PUBLIC LIBRARY

"HUGGING AND SLUGGING"

Madison Square Garden is crammed and full of smoke. Gate keepers try to bustle us by, [and] broad shoulders clear the way in fine style. We get to an enclosure except by courtesy at box (no. 26) and find we can see well. After some light play among little ones and a very fine show by "Jimmy Kelly[24] and Tom Allen"[25] the event comes off. Sullivan[26] was a mass of muscle but Laflin[27] looked decidedly flabby and evidently lacked confidence but that was not remarkable as it is his first appearance in the ring. His blows had nothing like the power of Sullivan's though the latter hits round every time and is very clumsy. And the first time he meets a good man of his own size he will be beat for certain. This was a feeble performance and after they hugged one another for four rounds the referee gave the fight to Sullivan who was immediately challenged by "Paddy Ryan."[28] They do not fight till January. [I] received [a] letter and photo from Katherine and get a present of a small dog from Jaffray.[29] [I] hear there is a warrant out against me for the ducks [I stole] on the other side. I wish them luck.

    <u>Fine Drink</u> Fill a wine glass with crushed ice. Fill up nearly to the top with Kummel[30] and put a teaspoonful of old Brandy on top and eat ice and all. Sullivan is a fraud. Jimmy Kelly [is] the cleanest hitter I have seen yet. <u>Jerry Murphy</u>.[31]

[The following corroboration is written by John Frizzle.]
Monday
10th November 1884
Hoffman House New York
Very fine morning started after breakfast with Heygate and Evelyn to bank from there to gun makers. Evelyn Booth bought sharp rifle.[32] [I] inspected [a] lot of guns they had some lunch I did not take any [we] get back by elevated railway to Hoffman. I walked over to Brunswick House[33] with Evelyn [and] got letters from Mrs. Hammond[34] and "<u>Burggins</u>." Had something to eat and drink [and] walked back to Hoffman, wrote letters, dress for dinner 8 o'clock go and see boxing exhibition at Madison Square Garden.

    8.30 – Fiddler Neary[35] of New York fights Jack Keenan of Philadelphia.[36] [I] don't think very much about Neary. Keenans (meddling) (well

John L. Sullivan (1858–1918) is recognized as the first heavyweight champion of gloved boxing and held the title from 1882–1892. LIBRARY OF CONGRESS

built). 8.45 Joe Fowler, Featherweight Champion of England,[37] fights George Young the latter fast but more science about Fowler.[38] 9 o'clock. Tom Allen and Jimmy Kelly fight. I must say this was the best fight I ever witnessed. Both [had] plenty of science and [are] very fast. Kelly gets the best of it.

9.15 Jack Dempsey,[39] Champion Lightweight pugilist of America, fights Tom Ferguson[40] of Philadelphia the fight I don't think much of. 10 o'clock the event of the evening comes off. John L. Sullivan, the Champion of the World, fights Prof. John H. Laflin. Sullivan gains the day. Laflin has science on his side though beaten [in the] third round. Laflin [is a] much taller man then Sullivan but not as well made (Billy Edwards,[41] Laflin Second).

Yanks opposite our box next to us [are] very anxious about betting. After boxing, [we] come back to Hoffman [and] have Sandy Drinks.[42] Evelyn and Heygate go off to [a] gambling shop [and] I return to Hoffman with Sir George Beaumont[43] and drink whisky till very late find I get very complicated after 4th whiskey.

Up about 10.30 [and] find I am all by myself Heygate appears with [a] sponge and towel in hand. Have talk with him for some time he goes and has bath. I have breakfast in bed [with] no sign of the missing one (Evelyn Booth). Have great crack with Miss Bridget Butler.[44] She tells me that Mr. Booth is the warmest she ever "view'd" and also the most notorious blackguard.

P.S. Mrs. Burgess calls on me in the morning [to] talk with her for a long time and pass the officer up the body.

[The following entry is written by Evelyn Booth.]
Tuesday
11th November 84.
Hoffman House New York
About 4 p.m., I am roused by the entrance of the other devils and hear that all the detectives in New York are on my back. First impressions of the tongue business jam. Miss Evelyn Bell's[45] is the first house [and] she ought to be looked after. Frizzle has Reginald's lady after he goes and

attempts a rape on "Lulu."[46] The two had visited the police station and many other houses before finding me. After dinner, [I] go round to Read's and get completely cleaned out. Reginald comes in and does ditto. [I] think it a bad game and swear off. [I] have a long talk with Jacob, Head Detective. He says, he thought I was knocked on the head.

[There is a] Tosser[47] in distress [with a] severe application of alcohol the soft fellow wants touching up again. [We] storm the elevator at 1 p.m. and have an aerial flight in it. [To] great consternation among the night porters, [the] elevators [are] gone and the landing doors locked. I forgot to mention that 13 bottles of Pommery were consumed by the party at W. 74 W. 36th.[48] First rate breakfast in bed there sad to say the waiters tumbled to the dodge with our Kummel and watch us like mice. Think it better to try [the] ladies room again, the waiters are elderly there and look without guile, have discovered some good fizz at Del's.[49] Is it that nice man! Recipe for eating oysters: Put on them a little horse radish sauce and salt and pepper mixed.

Friday
Nov 14.
Find Reginald with a good old British head on him for the first time. He even refuses ginger. Mamie appears and looks very nice. She bolts at the sight of the drawers. [I] knockout Bridget with a well directed shot with Reginald's sponge which he has left behind. Jack[50] the only one who can face breakfast, Reginald [is] discharging bile at a great rate. He goes to bed again after embileing Brom.[51] We are suddenly seized by pugilistic ardor and send for gloves. The furniture had better be insured on the spot. We all retire to bed early [and] very cheap and come to the conclusion that the sooner we leave this city the better both for health and pocket. [We] shall leave for Niagara on Monday? But, [we] cannot settle on [the] route. Reginald thinks of a scheme for making money by advertising that he will swim the rapids. [He] is only afraid that they will want him to up first. Agent of West Shore[52] Log: "Well I guess I'll fix you up as nicely as you can be fixed."

[The following entry is written by John Frizzle.]
Nov 15. 84.
Hoffman House
After breakfast go down by elevated railway to Central Park Heygate, myself and Evelyn; beautiful morning. The first thing which attracted our attention is a snake of very small breed. This gives Heygate the alarms who is not well after the night. The snake is quickly dispatched by Evelyn and we proceed further through the park. The next thing which we discover are some quail close to the road in some bushes they soon take their departure and we proceed on our journey to a place called 'the cave' which is not very interesting. In this spot a very small beetle of some sort crosses Heygate's path, again he is seized with the "alarms" and jumps right off the road. A carriage is seen and Heygate takes possession of it telling the driver to take him to 66 Street the abode of his fowl.

Evelyn and myself turn back through the Park while sauntering along we notice numbers of nests through the trees not knowing what they are, our curiosity overcomes us with stone in hand we soon satisfy ourselves by finding that the Grey Squirrel is the owner, and a very fine little animal he is! There are numbers of them about this place in the park and we give chase to several, one very nearly getting it's deathblow by a large "paver" thrown by your humble servant (JPF).

We get back to Hoffman by 2 o'clock and have lunch. Heygate returns after seeing his fowl. [There is] great excitement among the New York Sportsmen at the Mayors action in prohibiting the coming fight.[53] 5 o'clock [the] first gloved contest between Evelyn and myself. 5.30 dress for dinner. Dr Wright[54] arrives at 6.30 [we] have the batch and any amount of Kummel [we] go over to Del Monicos after and begin on champagne. Drink away till 10.30 and smoke cigars. Heygate turns in and joins us getting very far gone. All three get into [a] cab and drive to New York hospital to Dr. Wright's room we go and drink whiskey in great form. After finishing his whiskey, which was very good, he leaves us some of the way home. Reginald [is] very much sprung and myself just as bad, a lot worse according to [our] acts.

[The following entry is written by Evelyn Booth.]
Sunday
Nov. 16. 84.
The usual aimless morning is enlivened by a spirited set between Reginald and Doc. Both very much blown at the end of 2 minutes. [I] take Eileen[55] out as far as the East River and see a lot of boys fishing and catching nothing. Coming back [I] nearly faint at the smell of the morgue. Would not go inside for 500 pounds – Reginald has no control over his <u>sphincter</u>. [I] spend [the] afternoon making list of necessaries for the West. Thanks be to the Lord the war among the railways is so great we can go all the way to Omaha quite close to Denver for 11 dollars. Probably it will be 5 tomorrow so these Jay Gould's[56] are useful

Fred Archer (1857–1886) was one of the most famous horse jockeys of the late nineteenth century. LIBRARY OF CONGRESS

sometimes. Find some useful hints for camp life in "Camps in the Rockies"[57] published in the field some time ago. Reginald [is] in tribulation at [a] message from home saying "Await important letters!!!" Letters must follow and take their chance.

Paragraph in [the] *New York Herald* saying Archer[58] is on his way out. Wonder what this means and wish he had been in time to ride at Jerome Park.[59] Our tame doctor when drunk boldly expressed his intention of having a ride this morning but thinks better of it. We say his travels in America would have probably ended abruptly. Sullivan and Greenfield were both arrested yesterday but let out on bail. Their case will not be settled till three tomorrow so nobody knows anything till the last minute. Have heard no betting so far. Public faith in "John" evidently [is] beginning to waiver after his last exhibition.[60] [I] had the first bad dinner here as yet last night but in the fault of an incompetent waiter.

Try new fizz, Vin brut.[61] I am horrified at finding the name of "Max Greges"[62] on the cork. [I] cannot make out what to do with [the] superfluous baggage as we may not come back here. The barber says he thinks I shall have a bigger moustache by the time I get back. Find we shall have a lot of useless clothes but determine to take the lot to Denver. After dinner [I] wander about the streets with Reginald in a vain attempt to find Miss Hastings[63] but as we have forgotten both the number of the street and the house it is necessarily an unsuccessful one.

[We] return and consult the dictionary and renew the search with Frizzle. We finish up at 74 W 76 and drink 7 bottles. Try another piece, she will not kiss it but she is very nice. Miss Burgess [is] still looking very bad. Frizzle astonishes the ladies by showing them the chair trick.

Monday
Nov 17.
Return [at] 9 a.m. and find Frizzle gone. I hear from Reginald that he got up too late to [get] breakfast with his friend the doctor and cursed the unlucky boy unmercifully. [The] mail [comes] in [with] nothing but a couple of wretched circulars [and] find on looking at [the] date they have been here for a week. Go round with Reginald and buy huge supplies of

Niagara Falls, NY DENVER PUBLIC LIBRARY

waterproofs and have a great time interweaving agents of N.Y. Central, decide on West Shore and take tickets as far as Chicago with liberty to stop at Niagara as long as we like. Try a new place for lunch (frightfully hot) and then to Wall Street and back by train to Union Square. Reginald bolts in pursuit of a "petticoat." [I] find Frizzle stripped packing like a devil. This is the only pursuit he shows any interest in but in the former case there was a bit of a salt to account for ardor.

Reginald rushes in [and] swears the lady is a "Christer," bolts a dose of brandy and is off to 341 East 19. [I] go around with Billy Edwards, and meet again Col. Early,[64] Arthur Chambers of Philadelphia,[65] Donovan[66] and a lot more. [I] take an affectionate farewell of Billy Edwards and go around with Jacob.[67] After several drinks at various faro houses, we finish up at 108 W. 31.[68] Champion place for ladies. Jacob gets blind and I leave him there at 4.30 a.m.

Fight postponed till Tuesday. We have waited a week to see it and get done. Also, [I] lose 75 dollars cost of 3 boxes.

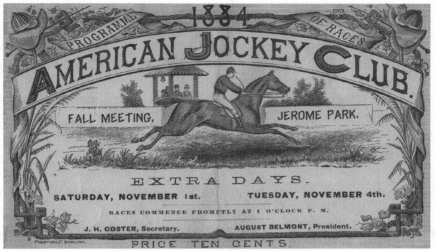

Horse racing program for Jerome Park in Bronx, NY DENVER PUBLIC LIBRARY

Tuesday
Nov. 18. 84.

Leave Carrie with regret and go back to Hoffman. Find Frizzle as usual asleep and have great difficulty in getting him out. Say goodbye to Bridget who presents me with an "Agnus Dei"[69] and 2 medals which are to bring me luck wherever I go. Leave Hoffman at 9.30 and drive to ferry at 42nd street. The new sooner is fond of Eileen.[70] Another one with a head like a bulldog appears at the ferry. The people here are evidently very proud of him. [The] wind [is] very cold crossing the river, first breath of winter we have had.

Start about 10.20 [there is] no drawing room car on [the] train. At first, [we] pass through a splendid looking place for wild fowl for some way when we change and get into the fast train. We go along close by the Hudson which is here I should say at least a mile wide with high bluffs on the other side. Stop at Kingston[71] for 10 minutes for lunch which is good though rather a scramble and very cheap. We run parallel with the NY Central and have a race with one of their trains. We come in second. [The] car [is] very comfortable and [the] attendants [are] most obliging. [There is] ice on pools by the side of the track.

No animal life of any sort. Stop twenty minutes for dinner at Syracuse, lots to eat and fairly cheap. Frizzle is greatly excited at the sight of a couple of polls. Sleep nearly all the way to Buffalo where we are chucked from the car we have been in and go into a common one. Only stop once between Buffalo and the Falls where we arrive at 1.30 and find a sharp frost. After collecting baggage, start in bus for Goat Island Hotel where we ordered [a] room but fail to rouse anyone.[72] So, [we] make for [the] Spencer House where we find shelter.[73] While waiting at G.I.H[74] [I] run down and look at [the] river but can see little but a rushing mass of white water. The noise is nothing like what I expected. Go to bed after a go at Reginald's old brandy which comes in useful on occasions like this. Find we paid 3 ½ dollars for tickets which is very severe as our tickets the whole way to Chicago are only $5, Pullman and all. Think I shall be very sick of trains by the time we go to Denver.

Reginald has taken Eileen to bed with him and the poor devil is making the night miserable with her howls in the lower regions.

Wednesday
Nov. 19
Niagara
After a rattling good breakfast leave in carriage to have a look at the celebrated falls, accompanied by Eileen. Go first and see [the] American falls from Prospect Park.[75] Then go down in a hydraulic arrangement (very jumpy business) and see it from below. A lot of ice about as there have been several days hard frost. A dense cloud of spray is rising from the Horse Shoe Falls and blowing over the trees on the Canadian side covering everything with ice looking lovely. Leave American side and cross by new suspension bridge getting a fine view up and down the river. The "Bridal Veil" has been utilized to work a lot of mills on the American side which do not add to the beauty of the prospect. Go down to the whirlpool rapids passing the cantilever railway bridge and old suspension bridge. Our driver has got the whole account of it by heart even to the number of strands of wire used in its construction. When you see the rapids the only wonderful thing is how Webb[76] ever got so far and how unlucky he was not to get himself into the whirlpool itself where we arrived five minutes later.

Prospect Park flanks Niagara Falls on the American side and provides spectacular views of the Falls. LIBRARY OF CONGRESS

We watched a dead horse floating round for some minutes. It was never taken under for more than a few seconds. [I] intend to go and have rifle practice at it tomorrow if [it's] there still. There were quantities of gulls all the way from here to the falls. Go up to "Table Rock"[77] on the Canadian side. Clouds of spray which turn into ice immediately envelop the whole place. Reginald dresses in oil skins and goes down to get behind the falls. We decline and look for drinks. After Reginald's return we drive up to the Burning Spring[78] H2S beastly stink and little else. I must confess to being disappointed with Niagara. It is a perpetual "50 cents please gents" and being bothered to buy bad photographs and Indian curios which look Brummagem. I think however we have got off lightly so far. Being so late in the year, we have missed all the Indians and [the] crowd of tourists. We saw some photos of sweet Gougers with the Falls as a background and resisted without difficulty the importunities of several gentlemen to get taken in the same way. Get back and have some oysters and go down to Goat Island. Meet a sportsman outside (proprietor) who entices us into the bazaar but buy nothing. Reginald however falls madly in love with a young lady who shows us round and gives him one of her own bracelets in hopes of getting something afterwards.

The rapids above the falls are very fine also the ones below the whirlpool. Great demonstration in honor of Cleveland.[79] Fireworks and revolvers going off in all directions and all the ladies of Niagara [are] on the prowl. They are the best looking lot taken as a whole that I have ever seen and up to anything.

[The following corroboration is written by John Frizzle.]
I corroborate this account of our day's proceedings. What left for me to say is little. The Horse Shoe Fall is very beautiful especially when seen from the Canadian side. The trees here are a fine site indeed with the frozen spray adhering to their branches. The part I liked most was the whirlpool no one who has not seen Niagara Falls have any idea of the vast stretch of water seen in this place. Our guide, who is a very good one, told me that no one truly appreciates Niagara who has not seen it in [the] winter and I quite agree with him. There was nothing particular occurred after we arrived home. When dinner was over I strolled out and find the town in a state of frightful confusion and excitement about Cleveland's election. Tar barrels burning effigies and omnibuses also are the order of the evening and [I] see Reginald and go try to pick up some of the Niagara fowl. Have no difficulty in this way the girls here are all for it.

[The following entry is written by Evelyn Booth.]
After breakfast walk to Goat Island and wander about by ourselves. Come to the conclusion that the finest view is to be had here. We get a real good view of the American Falls. It is rather jumpy going down to the point as all the steps are covered with ice. We then go and see the Horse Shoe from all points. There does not seem to be nearly so much spray today and the immense body of dark green water in the centre, where it takes

its final plunge, looks grand. Thence up to the rapids above which look like a stormy sea, there are numbers of ducks flying about but not near enough for us to tell what species. Start off after having some oyster to the whirlpool for revolver practice. Both [of] the dogs [are] with us go over the new suspension bridge from which we get a fine view of the rapids. When we get to our destination after firing a few shots from the upper platform we descend a great many steps to get to the water's edge. After a couple more shots we discover "Eileen" is gun shy.

We do not make brilliant practice and ascend 346 steps again. Very fatigued before we get to the top. Come back and make inquiry at driver's depots about starting tonight. Find we can start from the place we arrived at on Tuesday night [and] carriage hire is wonderfully cheap here. A good carriage and hire for the whole day for 2 dollars and the driver is glad of the smallest gratuity and thankful. Reginald comes back from seeing his lady, who he swears is perfection. She has however, stuck him for eleven dollars which takes off the guilt a little. The only sign of animal life on Goat Island was two white rabbits which bolted into a wall. The Dr. also spotted an old paper wasps nest at the far corner.

CHAPTER THREE

Hunting Thrills and Buffalo Bill

We left Niagara Falls at least the American side of the falls at 1 in the morning. Before leaving, Eileen had got into trouble which is a great nuisance after crossing by [the] old bridge we have to wait for 1 ½ hours on the Canadian side for a west shore train. Reginald employs the time getting light and making speeches in the refreshment room. Our sleeping car is attached on here. By the way, the attendants of these sleeping and drawing room cars are the only civil people connected with American railways. They are all blacks.

I am the first to wake and find we are passing through what must have been a great wood some time ago, as stumps of trees stick up everywhere in the small cleavings [sic]. We stop a few minutes at Chatham.[1] I luckily get some breakfast. The others who are still asleep have to wait several hours. Reach Detroit in about 1 ½ hours and have to cross in a ferry from [the] Canadian side to [the] American side. [There is] nothing to eat here and no drawing room car on the train to our disgust. Reginald and the Dr. have a light breakfast on apples. It is the most uninteresting country to travel through perfectly flat and nothing to look at except those hideous snake fences. At a small place just beyond Auburn[2] we stop for dinner which is fair. You never saw three fellows put away so much in such a short time. There has been a lot of ice about all the way and at one place we see a lot of ducks.

Arrive at Chicago tired out at 9 p.m. and drive to Palmer House,[3] the largest hotel in America? It is on the American plan. And they feed us and give us real good rooms with baths attached for the same price as our rooms alone were at New York. [Go] to bed early.

Sat.

Nov. 22 84.

Chicago Ill.

After breakfast, go forth to Thomas's, gun maker, but he is not in. On the way [I] see a miserable object dragged out of an eating house by two officers. He has some bad looking bruises but curls up in [the] bottom of [the] cart as if he was used to it. Go round to Cook's[4] but extract no information. Go and have oysters and broiled lobster with chili sauce, real good. Find Thomas in on our return. He is most obliging but puts a stopper on our ideas of going west by saying unless we get a pass from General Sheridan[5] to Barnett[6] we have no chance of elk or grizzly. He wires to some pal of his in Sioux City[7] to give us the address of "Boney Ernest"[8] and to know if [there is] any chance of sport.

Mean time he says we shall get any amount of ducks and deer in "Arkansaw" and later on, thousands of snipe[9] in Texas. This sounds good. Discover that I have been shooting shells of the wrong caliber out of my revolver which accounts for their bursting. This city is a year in front of New York as far as pavements and streets, and the tramways are apparently run by electricity and go a hell of a pace. Thomas came to dinner and afterwards we went out to see some of the sights of Chicago. Telegram from Saint Louis about "Arkansaw" *send party along [and] will guarantee them as many ducks, deer, and wild turkeys as they can shoot at.* Go round to gambling shop. I win, also Reginald, but the Dr. loses. Reginald and I proceed to the nearest bawdy house. We intend to stay all night but come to the conclusion it is not alright and retire. Reginald has some view of a woman defecating. Go to bed blind.

[The following entry is written by John Frizzle]

Sunday

Nov. 23.

Evelyn very bad after night get the reliable drought but it only acts as emetic. Reginald in about 10.30 he goes off to meet Thomas he complained of. Woke in the morning and find it snowing and a hard frost. Stay in the morning and talk harsh to the little chamber maid. She comes from Christiana.[10] The cowboy band plays downstairs and very well too.

They hail from Dodge City, Kansas and are attired in the cowboy costume. They all carry highly ornamented six shooters with one of which, Captain, keeps time. Go to bed early still very cheap. The theaters here are just the same as any other day.

[The following entry is written by Evelyn Booth.]
Monday
Nov. 84.
Get up early and find thermometer [reads] 6 below zero 38 degrees of frost icicles hanging from the horse's bits and bitter wind. After breakfast, the cattlemen parade to the station on the way to the stockyard [and] spend all the morning shopping and get everything except the cook. Put [an] advertisement in [the] paper. Buy tremendous assortment of knives and Reginald disposes of his old one to the doctor for 8 dollars. [It is] snowing hard. We have brought two barrels of Scotch whisky which is the nearest to Poteen[11] I have ever tasted. Hear [a] glowing account of game in "Arkansaw" but a poor one of the ladies. Go around and speculate at Faro, Reginald wins a little. See fire brigade on [the] road [and] they seem to be going very slow. Then start for Carrie Watson's 441 South Clark.[12] [There are] any amount of ladies but rather aged. Reginald goes off with one very quick and swears he will stay all night.

Before arriving at 441 we have astonished Thomas by the rate we dispose of brandy cocktails, Santa Cruz Rum, etc. Retire after a concert and am immediately joined by Reginald's lady. She has enough paint on to "Paint the town red." A fat French woman then comes and is very anxious to kiss it. My original piece is very nice she comes from Alabama [and] styles herself a "Johnny Reb" and hates the yanks.

Leave 441 with a broken finger, cut head and contused shoulder.

Tuesday
Nov. 25.
Engage servant and go see my sticking place. The gentleman who wielded the knife did it as if he loved them. It takes two minutes to convert a live "muck" into sausages. Have [a] wretched dinner at Chapin and Gores[13] and struggle at Faro at 125. Win $600 between us. We like Faro. Go

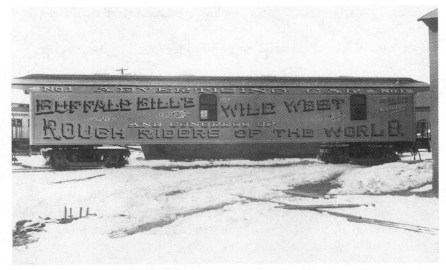

This train car, ca. 1893, is the style of car Buffalo Bill may have used.

round to Coon houses, French Emma's[14] and a lot more places. Break the lot tossing. One lady plaintively exclaimed, "You might give me back my quarter." She had extracted the aforesaid quarter from the bottom of her stocking. Reginald gets sucked by a damsel very like Gussie. She swallowed the lot. He also tosses a fat woman 4 dollars against her body, wins but does not use his advantage. Win two bottles of fizz from Bell Demmick.[15] Old Thomas is beginning to get weak. The Dr. has given him 1 ½ days longer to live. If he takes a prescription the Dr. has given him. I allow him less. The ladies here are inferior to New York but every house seems to be a knocking shop. Go and have dinner with Gunn the gambler.

There is a dish called Spanish Stew[16] which is excellent. Meet old sportsman from Denver. He says there is still big game near there. A little gouger is mad to take us on at Faro and even proposes [to] come to St. Louis and play $1,000. We decline with thanks. Meet Patrick Sheedy,[17] Sullivan's backer, he has come on purpose to tackle the English strangers. We begin to think Chicago is getting rather worn and are not sorry when we leave the Aeton depot at 9 p.m. for St. Louis.

Train [is] crammed. We have good baths but do not sleep well, having heard so much about thieving lately. Take on Reginald at 25 cent Faro and come off quits.

[The following corroboration is written by John Frizzle.]
Monday
24. November
Palmer House
After breakfast, went downstairs saw the cowboys and their band, they played in great style in [the] hall of Palmer House police on the job headed by their Lieutenant they look a hardy lot of devils. As for the cowboys, don't think much of them. Reginald got great friends with one of them and produced some of his best cigars much to the Cowboys delight. After they played a time in the hall, they marched off three days. Reginald, Evelyn and myself went down to see Thomas, gun maker, looked at a lot of guns and gave orders. Went off then to buy whiskey old "stick in the mud" Thomas accompanies us [and] get what we want in that line. Reginald leaves us and Evelyn and myself go to Baltimore and Ohio Depot where we have remainder of luggage; get them. All night and travel back to gun makers. [It is] very cold indeed.

[The following entries are written by Evelyn Booth.]
Nov. 27. 84
St Louis, MO
We arrive at this place at 8 a.m. and after the usual struggle after baggage, drive to the Southern Hotel[18] and start on the severe undertaking of shunting useless things. The Dr. is very cheap and even the prospect of "packing" does not awaken him. The depot was full of "hunters" and their smell dogs us. This is Thanksgiving Day and is a general holiday. Agent of Texas Railway introduces himself [and] recommends Weiner[19] but knows very little about the country. It is quite hot here thermometer at 70, such a change to Chicago which we left in a heavy snow storm. All water here is dark brown in spite of all the filters which have been erected at great expense. Before leaving Chicago rushed and had final go at Faro and copped $80 dollars. The Mississippi is nothing like the mighty river

I expected and the steamboats by no means the floating palaces they are painted. Spend ½ hour in rifle and pistol practice and make good shooting with Stevens .22 pistol.[20]

This seems a deadly place and not even a straight Faro bank. Play pyramids[21] with Reginald on [a] table with pockets like ditches. After Thanksgiving dinner, rarely attempt to find <u>Vie De Mais</u>.[22] Gambling is a penitentiary crime in this city. Go to bed early. [It is] raining hard.

Friday
Nov. 28.
"St. Louis," MO
Have [a] long interview with agent of railway and take tickets for Fisher.[23] Leave St. Louis at 3 p.m. and after a miserable journey arrive at Fisher at 10 the next day 3 hours late.

Saturday
Nov. 29
In Camp Fisher, Ark.
Fix up the tent and start off on the hunt. The wood is very thick and we walk about six miles and only see one lot of ducks very wild. Go in another direction and find some quail in thick cover. They are the hardest bird to hit in a wood I ever seen and a good deal of wild shooting only brings three to the bag. Go back to camp and find the Dr. and Reginald have bagged five parrots and a huge owl. Retire to bed early intending an early start for Swan Lake,[24] which according to all accounts swarms with duck.

Sunday
Nov. 30.
Get up at six after an uncomfortable night and have [a] good breakfast. Mule team and wagon appears and the driver looks, and is, a real Scotty. We christen him Sandy on the spot. He informs us we shall be fined for shooting on Sunday. This we ignore and start off up the railway track while he follows the road. We beat both sides of the track and get some good shooting at quail and mallard. The doctor shoots a filthy buzzard

which he swears is a condor. He proceeds to dissect it on the spot. We reach Weiner (10 miles) some time before the wagon and buy some luxuries at the store. He kept beer but had been drunk out the day before. We leave for Swan Lake after frugal meal and get somewhere near in about an hour. Reginald was beating about for quail when a big deer jumped up right under his nose but 2 barrels of no. 7 failed to stop him. Find a good place to camp and walk out to have a look at the lake. See any amount of ducks flying about but all out of shot. While supper is cooking, thousands of ducks fly over towards the swamp but [are] very high.

Dec 1.
In Camp Swan Lake
We have got into the way of making things comfortable and all sleep well in spite of the howls of a "panther" which prowls round all night. Get up at six thirty and am just late for the morning flight. The Dr. and I explore the swamp after breakfast and see thousands of all kinds of game, swans and ducks of every kind. Kill a good many mallard, wood duck and teal. The swamp is very hard to get through but not dangerous. See some swans but not in shot. It is a real bad place to pick up game as there is so much water if you do not kill everything stone dead you have no chance to find it and if you brought a dog it would have to swim all the time. Go down to the swamp with Reginald for the evening flight shoot till our guns are red hot. The air is absolutely alive with ducks and the noise of their wings is like a cotton mill. We knock down forty but cannot pick them up as it is black dark before we leave we have a hard job to get home. Last night Sandy gave us a lecture on the merits and demerits of Queen Elizabeth!!! This is a wild fowl paradise!!! There was ice on the water bucket this morning but it got very warm in the middle of the day.

Dec. 2nd 84.
In Camp Swan Lake
Out by myself all the morning [and] shot 10 ducks, never saw such a great quantity of ducks before. [I] went down to the bottom of Swan Lake. Went on the prowl for a deer and took a long circuit but saw nothing but

some stray duck and one bevy of quail till quite close to camp when just as I had taken out my cartridges up jumped a deer right under my nose and went off in a succession of jumps. More ducks than ever but not so much shooting. All the ones we left yesterday had been eaten up by some devils, I suspect buzzard.

Dec 3. 84.
Sharp frost this morning, [and] ice half an inch thick. Send Sandy on mule back to Fisher to look for 8 bore cartridges. He has slight difference with the mule at starting and the services of the Dr. are called into requisition. Go off in a new direction with the Dr. and find plenty of duck but most infernal place to pick them up. We follow this creek for a long way and killed about 30 principally wood duck. Then come back and go down to the big swamp but there are so many together that it is hard to get near them. See some geese and swans cross a very ugly looking place by means of a beaver dam and get back very tired and spend the afternoon skinning wood duck and setting things to straights. A gentleman from another camp has ridden over hearing of our Dr. He is afflicted with weeping eczema. Reginald gets in a great state as he has been riding his horse round. Soon afterwards another gentleman arrives. He turns out to be the sub sheriff. He inquires if we have licenses and evidently hopes to stick us for $10 dollars but we do not tumble.

Dec. 4. 84.
Explore beaver creek again with the Dr. and kill some wood duck. Go across to town (Weiner) and find Reginald has just concluded a deal for two ponies, wagon and cover. Have long conversation in the store with [a] gentleman who has just served two years for killing a man. He said it was a very pretty fight. This was his third man. We taste beer for the first time since we came out. Reginald buys another pony, an old white mare. After our return to camp the Dr. shoots a small pig and cuts it up. He is haunted by its companions all night. It comes on to rain at six and continues hard at it all night and the whole place resembles a lake in the morning so we make up our minds to move further on. – The last of Balmoral – [25]

Grouse—examples of game killed on a hunt DENVER PUBLIC LIBRARY

Dec 5th 84.

Get to Weiner ourselves all right but the ponies get stuck and have to make two trips. So fix camp close to railway. The whole place is so wet we have to lay down boards to sleep on. Get tossing a lot of loafers for drinks and get blind. Have great success tossing at poker dice.

Dec. 6. 84.[26]

Weiner, AR

Very cheap after [the] night and don't get up early. Darkie comes along the track [and] says he has been boycotted higher up and has had nothing to eat for two days. The Dr. makes him earn a dinner by chopping wood and washing our dirty clothes. Weiner is a terribly dirty place. Buffalo Bill[27] departs for Brinkley[28] by the morning train. His whole pack of dogs follow the train but return soon. Have a miserable cold night on a plank bed and am roused by the return of Buffalo Bill at 4 a.m. He can be heard God Damning everything and everybody.

Dec. 7. 84.

Sharp frost and we determine to start south. The Dr. and I strike into the wood on one side and Buffalo Bill and Reginald go on the quail interest on the other. Bill has announced his intention of killing every bird he fires at, but we are not surprised to hear that out of seven shots he failed to hit anything and departed cursing awfully. On our way the Dr. kills five quail at one shot but we see no large game at all. Hear terrible account of Devil's garden. They say no dog ever came out of it alive. We hope to sample it tomorrow. A man who had been missing for 48 hours was found today. He had gone mad and torn off all his clothes and hid in the bushes from the men who were looking for him. Find Fisher a much more comfortable place to camp than Weiner. The Dr. has made friends with an old Irish settler. He invites us all to supper. A lot of loafers, as usual, hanging about the depot (bums).

Dec 8th 84.

Start the wagon off in good time for Hickory Ridge[29] and adjourn to dinner with Mrs. Maloney.[30] She gives us an amount of delicacies and tells us a terrible tale of a tape worm which ate up one of her children. I was afraid it was going to be produced as she talked of it being kept in a bottle somewhere. After the Dr. had eaten the whole of a huge cake, we start to face the Devil in his den. Reginald has encircled himself in several belts and knives beside a huge Winchester. He earns the sobriquet of "Texas Jack." We fail to find anything more terrible than squirrels and rabbits in the Devil's garden and arrive at Hickory Ridge safe and find the team has not yet arrived. In the course of an hour it appears with two oxen as leaders and we proceed to search for a place to camp. Meanwhile, the wagon has stuck in a hole and when "Dave and Bully" fail to draw it out (through their driver who is a splendid chap [and] tries all he knows). Before it gets dark we have to stop where we are for the night. It is not such a bad spot except there is no water but we light a huge fire and are fairly comfortable. Very cold night.

Dec 9th 84.
Dave and Bully appear and pull us out quick and we start from Hickory Ridge for Tilton[31] to which they say is distant seven miles. The road is hard to find for the first mile, but quite hard, and Reginald rattles the ponies along at a great pace. After we have traveled at least six miles we come to a settler's house. The men as usual lean over the gate and stare and say nothing. We have never seen a back woodsman put his to anything yet. They are all too lazy to milk their cows and to live on their hogs which run wild all the year in the woods. We inquire how far it is to Tilton and are told six miles!!!! This reminds one exactly of an Irishman's answer. After three hours more, we arrive at Tilton the road is very bad the last half slick just outside the place and have to get pulled out by mules. There is the usual hunter's camp by the track, it seems impossible to get away from them. There is a saloon here with the vile spirits but no beer. The other party have a fiddler among them and the Dr. dances an Irish jig for their amusement and Reginald shows them how to play whist.[32] Before we go to sleep the driver of Dave and Bully appears with some of his pals and they make use of the most filthy expressions for almost ½ an hour. This appears to give them great satisfaction, at least they laugh enough.

Dec. 10. 84.

Reginald starts off on the look for letters which have been following us about for the last month. He goes on a freight train so his return is doubtful. A head agent of the line is in the caboose with him and recommends "Hunter"[33] for deer, etc. . . . but it is just the same everywhere. They all say if you go to such and such a place you will find lots of deer and when we go there, there are none. I go out for a walk but it comes on to rain so I don't go far and see nothing but rabbits and squirrels. The wood is very thick nearly as bad as the Devil's garden and looks likely enough but is, I expect, hunted too much. Go and look for squirrels with the Dr. but they are gone scarce and we resort to rifle practice with the Sharp rifle. The bar keeper has been drunk all day and his saloon is closed. The other party killed a deer this morning so there must be some about. It comes to rain hard about seven and when Reginald comes back about nine he found us lying in a pool of water which is getting deeper as pitch but we luckily find a shed with some cotton bales [and] make ourselves as comfortable as circumstances permit. Find [a] tarantula spider in bed!!!

Dec. 11. 84.

Tilton, Ark.

Sleep well in spite of the Doctor's kicks and find it still pouring so we pack up intending to leave by the morning train. Have great trouble in making [a] fire but eventually succeed. Have several offers for the team but none come up to our standard so hire a coon to drive them to Brinkley for $5 dollars. I don't envy him his job as the roads will be terrible even for a light wagon after all this rain. The train is seven hours late having been again wrecked. This makes twice in four days. Reach Brinkley and get a poor dinner. It seems a miserable place. See three snipe within shot of the hotel door. Leave Gus and Dan[34] here and all the guns and leave for Hot Springs[35] at 10 p.m. Train as usual hours late. We have never yet seen a train "on time" in this country. Get to Little Rock[36] and find the Hot Springs train has waited for us. Reginald gets left, owing to difficulty with a baggage master whom he hauls out of his car by the legs. Reach Hot Springs at 5.30 a.m. and go straight to bed at Arlington Hotel[37] and sleep till eleven.

Dec 12. 84.

Hot Springs

Owing to all our respectable things having been left at St. Louis we have to appear in Shooting Costume which seems to amuse the natives not a little especially the Dr.'s boots which can be heard on the boards a mile off. We both have a hot bath but don't think much of it. Go up to [the] Depot with Eileen and meet Reginald who has had his beard removed at Little Rock and looks quite smart. We go to a saloon and have some real good brandy cocktails.

In the morning, I purchased a pair of boots and the coon who brought them informed me that his master kept a faro bank and also a boarding house where we could have as many women as we liked. After supper we go and have a turn at faro and win a bit but lose at another place at roulette. The proprietor pretends not to understand the game and Reginald tells him the only part he seems not to understand is the paying part. We eventually frighten him so much that he will pay on anything. After this, Reginald goes to bed but I proceed to look at the women accompanied by some gamblers. The fowl are very poor lot but anything goes down after such a long abstinence as ours.

Dec. 13th 84.

One of the gamblers Russell, alias White Pine,[38] comes down for me in a hack. He is very polite and evidently hopes to get something out of me. Go and have [a] bath and drink a lot of hot water which makes me very ill and spend most of the day in bed. Get [a] telegram from Bowling[39] saying he and Fred Archer are coming here. No baggage arrived yet. Reginald goes and has a lady at Shipley's.[40] Her age is something under sixty and the Dr. says he shaped round her like a dog. Go to bed without any faro as all very tired and read *Life of Jesse James*.[41]

[The following entry is a corroboration written by John Frizzle.]
Start off with Reginald and look after baggage but get no information about it. The offices which we go to are all closed up. No one seems to be about. Meet some of (Shipley's Crew) one Mr. Russell who does his best to drag Reginald into [a] gamble but soon finds that it is no go. He

asks also after Mr. Evelyn Booth and wants to know will he be about in the evening. We give him the slip and go rifle shooting to Daniel Barret's place.[42] Play general Hell with [the] show by breaking all his bottles. He calls us (Dandy shots). Reginald has a fowl the worst I ever saw, something like the "old bit at Cambridge" but [with] better teeth. Turn into Arlington and have dinner. The people are quite astonished at our dress especially my boots which make [the] wooden floors of the Arlington House sit up. After dinner, have the "crack" with Mr. J. Farin[43] who gives me great account of his life [and] how he caught snakes in South America and shot tigers in Africa. The people in the hall crowded round and took it all. He told me he was writing his life [story] and he would present me with a copy when finished. A hunter comes in with a large black spider which he has caught and calls it a tarantula one of the worst sort. I inform him that I killed one in our camp just as large only a week ago. He is much surprised and I am the same when I find out what their bile is for.[44]

Retire to our room No. 3. Reginald in bed with Eileen [and I] find night porter smoking [a] cigar and making himself quite at home. He wants to lend me a dollar till the morning but I decline the offer with thanks. Get the monster out of our room and give out the crack. Reginald retires to his room but not without stinking [up] the place with his H2S (Sulphurated Hydrogen).

[The following are written by Evelyn Booth.]
Dec 14. 84.
"Hot Springs"
Have breakfast brought to our room as this being Sunday we decline to face the public room in knickerbockers. We astonish the waiter by the amount we consume. Go and have a look at the springs where the hot water comes and afterwards have a turn at faro at Shipley's and both win a little. We seem to be the only players so I presume all the inhabitants are stony as the game is perfectly square. After tea, "Hullo Doc" comes in but meets with a rude rebuff from Reginald who fixes him with his cold gray one and he retires. Go and get beaten by Shipley at faro. The runs were something extraordinary and the only wonder was we did not lose more.

Example of men playing faro DENVER PUBLIC LIBRARY

Monday
Dec. 15. 84.
Pack the Dr. off to Brinkley to sack Gus and get things left there and try [a] new shop for faro on the way to meet Bowling and Archer at the depot. The train is punctual for once. They are not struck with the general appearance of Hot Springs. Take Fred to a faro place; he is immediately recognized by the proprietor. Reginald wins $75 dollars at roulette. Have a row with an old saloon keeper who swears lemonade is soda water. [I went] to bed early.

Tuesday
Dec. 16. 84.
Hot Springs Ark.
Telegram from Dr. saying nothing has been heard of [a] wagon yet but he means to wait till it comes. Reginald and Fred go out for a ride and Bowling and I accompanied by Sol[45] drive off to look for quail of which we are assured there are plenty. We go out about six miles over awful roads and look in different directions we see never a feather nor even a squirrel. The ground formation is quite different here all stones and no undercover at all and the steep little hills [are] thickly wooded. See some huge locusts which stick to the trees and explore with [a] long stick the depths of a

most inviting looking little stream and succeed in unearthing one fish about ¾ of a pound apparently a salmo fontinalis [sic].[46] There are also lots of minnows. On our return go and shoot bottles with Reginald and Fred and drink several pints of fizz. We all go and battle at faro which results in our complete defeat and we retire and get laughed at by the Capitan. While we were coming back from the quail hunt we met four scorchers evidently real Duchesses on horseback but did not make their further acquaintance.

CHAPTER FOUR

A Very Merry New Year

Wednesday
Dec.17. 84.
Said goodbye to Hot Springs without regret after a long bout of packing where we miss the Dr. greatly. We express all our guns and things for the night to Sulphur, Tex.[1] where Reginald, Fred and I propose to stop for one days duck shooting but the Captain goes straight through. Have a good dinner at Malvern[2] at [a] hotel kept by [a] widow. It has been freezing hard all day. Meet [an] English conductor on Pullman name sake of my own. He was at Eton[3] but bolted and seems to have tried his hand at everything, (Cattle ranching, detective in Chicago, dealer at faro bank). He had to leave the North through a lynching row and has been twice shot but not badly. He told us all about how the cheating is done at faro so we resolve to have no more. Have excellent dinner on car during the consumption of which we enter Texas where liquor may not be sold nor even the Police News N.B.[4] This is a free country. It makes them wild to say. I always heard this was a free country when they tell you this or that cannot be done. Our Eton friend when asked what sort of place is Sulphur replies briefly, "Like Hell." He has initiated us into the mysteries of "poker."

We bundle out at Sulphur and as the train moves off hear furious oaths proceeding from Reginald who has gone forward to look after Eileen. The cause is that the cursed Southern Express have taken out all our baggage at Texarkana[5] and stranded us with a lot of perfectly useless cartridge bags. Time 9 p.m. and a hard frost. The Captain has decidedly the right end of the stick now. However, somebody comes forward and gives us leave to leave the bags in a store of which he is foreman and also tells us of a place where it is possible to obtain a bed but advises us all to stick in one room. Get a darkie with a lantern to show us the way and obtain a room. Fred searches vainly for a bottle of fizz which ought to have been in his bag but which the Captain has extracted surreptitiously by and earns our hearty displeasure. However, we have half a flask of brandy which is consoling and arrange ourselves for the night two on the bed and one on the floor. Reginald and I have [a] great snoring match and abuse one another in the morning.

Thursday
Dec 18. 84.
Sulphur, Tex.
Very cold all night and snowing hard this morning. Have some fat pork for breakfast which Fred cannot tackle and plaintively exclaims, "You fellows must have stomachs like horses." Walk up to depot to catch 8 o'clock train. Train comes in and Reginald goes to leave Eileen in [the] baggage car. We see him turn away and cannot make it out and the train is gone in a second leaving us staring at one another. We discover with relief that it was not the one for Houston after all. Our friend of the night before who turns out to be English is very obliging and succeeds in getting us the loan of two guns armed with which we proceed to look for ducks after loading some cartridges. After walking some distance through a swampy place, we come to a bend of the "Sulphur River"[6] and see a big lot of ducks which get up very wild. We sit down on some logs while our guide and a darkie go up and down the river to keep them, the ducks, in motion. Only a few come back and we only knock down one which of course is taken by the current right to the other side. After waiting a long time and no more appearing, Reginald proceeds to attempt to cross on a raft of logs and gets over after some time and secures the duck and eventually gets back safe but not without losing his only pipe which sunk like a stone.

The old woman is mad at us for being late but comes round on being gently handled. The girl who waited on us refuses half a dollar offered by Reginald. Fred distinguishes himself by eating half a pineapple cheese and by trying a lot of chilies heat. Go up to [the] depot and hear the pleasing intelligence that our train is three hours late. "Jake"[7] again proves himself a true friend and takes us over to his house where we drink whisky and tell ghost stories. When the train arrives we determine not to get left and bundle on anywhere. Meet eventually in Pullman and get some beer from [an] attendant who is very civil but the fellow who examines the tickets tries to be nasty but we treat him with contempt.

Have [a] good breakfast on [the] car and arrive at Houston at 3 p.m. and drive to Capitol Hotel.[8] Here we recover our baggage but have to pay $33 dollars on it which we mean to try and recover. Fred is very cheap and goes to bed early. Reginald goes out and wins $240 dollars at faro. The proprietor says it is too thick and shies all the cards out of the box.

Dec 20. 84.

Houston

Go round and enquire about shooting at gun makers and buy [a] Smith and Wesson pistol 38 cal. Stroll round town with Fred Archer but find nothing of interest. It is very warm just like a hot house. Have [a] talk with a Pole he declaims like the rest against the "God Damn Country." After this, meet Reginald and all go and play faro. I manage to win after a hard struggle but Reginald loses. Reginald interviews [the] Captain of [a] tugboat who says Morgan's Point[9] and Lynchburg[10] are the best places and the boat starts at 9 tomorrow morning and reaches there in two hours. No news from Dr. yet. There is good whisky to be got here and Reginald gets some to send to Jake at Sulphur.

Dec. 21. 84.

Get down to tug [boat] in full force at 9 but she does not start till 10. The bayou is very narrow the first part and we see [a] good many turtle. There is another sportsman on board who gives a great account of the place. There are a lot of buzzards about but there is a $5 dollar fine for shooting one on account of them being public scavengers. We race another boat and win easily. Only see a few ducks on the way and some herons and small white cranes. On arriving at Lynchburg at 1 p.m. we leave our traps in [a] deserted shed and start off for snipe. Reginald kills one directly and Fred a dotterel.[11] We do not see another snipe till just as we are leaving this place attracted by the sound of heavy firing on the other side of the river by a German boy who appears to have his wits about him and

49

immediately find snipe. It is very wet and bad walking but we kill 17 snipe in a few minutes although there are 10 fellows blazing away all round.

There is a good store kept by and [sic] old German who says he can put us up the next time we come. The tug is late coming back and has a biggish craft to pull when it does appear. So we expect to get home late. The skipper has got his wife on board. She bests him at all points on an argument about American government. The sportsman who came down with us in the morning is very quiet as he has only killed two snipe. We get back at 10.30 and retire after [a] moderate supper upstairs. Reginald has lost his coat with all his keys etc.

Dec. 22. 84.
Leave by *Justine*[12] about eleven. The Captain nearly gets left but arrives at the last minute. We run aground for a few minutes but get off by lightening forward. See a small dead alligator. Arrive at Lynchburg rather late to do much good but kill 40 snipe and some other birds in about an hour. We had anticipated sleeping in an old shed but Fred had been foraging about and discovered a shanty belonging to the owner of the *Mollie Mohr*[13] where we can put up. They make us fairly comfortable and have splendid fires. They are "Dutch People." Have a good gamble at faro and read *Lives of the Queens of Folly.*[14]

Dec. 23. 84.
Start early, intending to have a great go at the snipe, but unlucky all [the way] through. It is a warm and muggy day and the smoke hangs tremendously and the light is very bad. Reginald and myself are the only shooters who stay out anytime. The bag amounts to 50 snipe and some ducks, quail and bittern.[15] There are a lot of the latter and they are easy to kill at least no. 8 fetches them at long distances. Come back covered with mud and have plunge in the river greatly to the astonishment of the natives who predict fever.

Dec. 24. 84.
"Lynchburg"
Start with Fred and Reginald for a final go at the snipe before leaving for Morgan's Point. Fred sits down in the mud before going far and soon

retires ditto [for] Reginald. I go on a bit further and find more than I have seen anywhere yet but I have only a few cartridges and run out after killing 16 [and] bag 20 snipe. The *Justine* is late coming down. On the way there is [a] great slaughter of "Poldoos" [sic] (coots)[16] and one heron.[17] We arrive at Morgan's Point at 6 p.m. and are warmly welcomed by the Captain's wife. She seems to have a nice place here though rather drafty and gives us a good dinner. It has turned very bad weather for duck shooting.

Morgan's Point, Tex.
Strong wind blowing and colder than ever. After breakfast, Reginald and Frizzle go up on the *Justine* to a place about four miles up. I depart with a darkie who funks the crossing and says we shall get soaked getting more than a little splashed. There are a good many ducks sitting about on the mud but very few on wing. The darkie says because of the cold. Stay about two hours and only kill a duck and a teal so [I] quit. After lunch, start again with Darkie to [a] place called Cedar Bayou where the ducks come in at night.[18] See any quantity but [am] very wary and only kill three all very long shots. Find on returning that Fred and Reginald have produced about a dozen as the result of their days work. Play all fours[19] and poker till bedtime.

Dec. 26th 84.
Much the same weather far too windy for boat work. Go out with [the] Captain to roosting place but ducks wilder than ever. Reginald kills two pelicans in the morning horribly ugly birds and perfectly useless. It comes on to thunder and lightning with heavy rain in the evening and goes on all night.

Dec. 27. 84.
Make an early start for Houston by *Justine*, rain still falling in torrents and very void. Lightning every minute. Kill pelicans, ducks, and heron on the way up and play nap. Find on our arrival at Capitol that the Dr. has at last turned up. Reginald is cheap and retires to bed early. Get some English letters. Fred, Doc and self went round to the skating rink but found only a lot of louts and no fowl. In the afternoon Fred and I drew several

Example of Buffalo Bill shooting glass balls thrown by Johnny Baker Credit
DENVER PUBLIC LIBRARY

bawdy houses but only found a lot of cows. Have sparring exhibition in the evening between Fred and Darkie. [A] Very near thing. Reginald in bed all day.

Dec. 29. 84.
Resolve to leave guns etc. and make a start for New Orleans. The Doc as usual [is] great at packing. Fred sneaks off and does a round of coon houses etc. by himself. Win $25 dollars at faro just before leaving. The storm still continues and the lightning is more frequent than ever. There is no liquor to be got on the car and the darkie is awfully anxious to get us to bed and equally so to get us up two hours too soon in the morning.

We arrive at New Orleans about 7.30 and have to leave cars and cross [the] river in [a] ferry. Eileen is forgotten and left in the baggage car. Get up to St. Charles Hotel[20] and have breakfast and stroll about. The streets are filthy, much of every description is in the gutters, and barely paved. Go up in a caravan to Buffalo Bill's Wild West Show in Oakland's Park.[21] The performance is simple but well managed. Bogardus[22] shoots some clay pigeons very feebly. Among the celebrities are "Buck Taylor,"[23] "Old Man Nelson"[24] the cowboy sheriff, and a lot of Mexicans and Indians. Buffalo himself shoots balls well while galloping past with a Winchester rifle. The roads on the way to Oakland's Park defy description. There are lots of orange trees in the gardens some of them covered with fruit. Nothing going on in the evening.

Dec. 31. 84.

Doc, Fred and self start for exposition in tram 5 cents all the way.[25] Go first to the Panorama of the Battle of Sedan.[26] Then to the main building. Fred gets weighed and scale [reads], 133 pounds.[27] The place is not finished and hardly any exhibits at all – no foreign one – and I think it extremely probable that it never will be. There is nothing whatsoever to see except some cotton machinery which we have seen in London years ago. There are some horses and ponies. Clydesdales, Normans, etc. and some fair cattle. Sol is in high delight at the prospect of going home. Get fair lunch at Exhibition (smart lot of waiters). It comes on to rain heavily about 4.30 and the trams back are crowded. They fill them up without any regard to numbers. After dinner, go round with Doc to faro place 32 Charles Street. After that, [go] to Park Theatre and Royal Street, a great place for keno.[28][There is] nothing, [to] pay at [the] Park Theatre except for drinks. There are some ladies of the lowest description but not so good as when we saw them in New York. The keno game is managed by electricity and appears to [be] a simple lottery. Play at grand hazard hearing there is no percentage against the player but very soon find out there is. Bands are promenading the streets in spite of the rain and crackers going off in all directions. We see the New Year in and go to bed about one. Reginald's throat is still bad and he stays in bed all day.

Jan 1. 85

New Orleans, La.

Great change in weather, quite cold. Am surprised to find Pemberton[29] has arrived from Cheyenne. He is two days late having been stuck in a swamp with nothing to eat. He has had no shooting at all. Went up with Pemberton to see Buffalo Bill's[30] show again, I fear the "Hon. Cody" is having a bad time of it as there are hardly any spectators and his expenses must be very heavy. Go to theatre in the evening to see *Monte Cristo*. Very feeble. On our return find there is a big fire close. The old wooden houses burn like matchwood and a whole block has been already consumed. The engines have nothing like the power of ours and there seems to be no system among the firemen.

Jan 2nd 1885
Lazy morning have breakfast in bed. Afterwards, go to Spanish fort with Cap, Doc and Fred. It takes about an hour by train through fine looking place for ducks. Fred roots up some alligators with a long pole and the Doc breaks a tiger cats teeth. They all make eyes at a piece in the train coming back but Fred the only one who ventures to address her, gets beautifully snubbed. Try new place for dinner (Madame Eugenie's[31] [sic]) cooking very good. Have [a] gamble and then Reginald does not stay long but I pass the night very pleasantly with a lady who reminds me strongly of Katherine.

Jan. 3. 85.
Arrive at home at 12 and find Reginald still in bed. Stay and talk to him for a bit when in comes Pemberton fresh from another lady who he says is very fine. Presently, in comes Fred who says he had a real "merry arsed" one and that Pemberton had taken on the old "Casekeeper."[32] Spend the whole afternoon going backwards and forwards to 32. Go to academy of music. The play is like a harlequinade[33] and makes us laugh very much. The Doc and Fred are raving about the pretty girls they have seen in the streets. Find Buffalo in bed very sulky in the evening. He has been to [the] dime museum and finished up by getting cleared out at 32.

Jan 4 to 11, 85.
New Orleans, La.
This is the record of a terrible week and I heartily wish I had never seen this town. The events hereafter related are not in chronological order but as they return to my somewhat misty vision. The principal and Johnson who keep the saloon opposite this occurred the day after Doc had a

Buffalo Bill Cody, John Nelson, Buck Taylor, and various Wild West Performers stand next to the Deadwood Stagecoach DENVER PUBLIC LIBRARY

fearful row with one of their dealers which terminated in his favor. The dinner however cost $500. Met a fellow from Texas all champion boozers, Reginald pals up greatly with one called Tom and they pass the following 3 or 4 days in various stages of inebriety [sic]. We have sampled nearly every restaurant and sporting house in the town and the Doc has distinguished himself by bilking several ladies. [We] have discovered that Pemberton has a marked preference for stout and elderly "Casekeepers" as we have always to send for the fattest ladies in the house.

There are a very feeble lot of "coons" here but lovely white girls. Reginald has discovered an angel who keeps a private carriage but only sticks to her for one day as he saw an angel in the balcony and promptly engaged rooms next door. The landlady is a pimp and offers to procure him an introduction but he has not got it yet. Find I have passed most of the week at Basin Street except one night which Pemberton, Fred and I passed at a shanty kept by a sportsman called "Nick Shamville"[34] at "Chef Menteur"[35] the latter place deserved it's [*sic*] name as we never got a shot although we went out in "pirogues after ducks at 3 a.m." The "pirogue" is a very narrow dug out liable to upset if you do not part you hair in the middle. And the mosquitoes were simply hell so we had by no means a pleasant trip and were devilish glad to be able to "jump a freight" on our return at 10 a.m. Fred had declined the hunt and gone back by the early train.

On Sunday went up with Reginald to see [a] fight [and] bet, seen Jerry Murphy and an unknown fighter who turns out a duffer and drunk to boot. It is stopped by the police and pronounced a draw. The steam train ran off the road just in front of us and smashed two cars up but nobody was hurt. At one time in the week we were in dire straits for money and both Reginald and self popped our watches!!! Fred and Doc went and shot with Johnson but did not get much. They all got full together afterwards. The Doc does a bilk on Laura all [the] while he and Fred and the Cap are watching. The tooth drawing [_____] comes up with a note from Miss Stanley requesting him to come and pay what he owes. The Doc nearly faints, he had previously met New York Minnie in the street and the Cap was greatly smitten. However he loses the good opinion he had previously of the Doc.

Jan 17th 1885

Thank goodness our remittances have arrived from New York and we can leave this horrid place. Regy has said goodbye to Lola and squeezed her behind the door which she objects to. We generally dine at Lopey [sic] now.[36] The waiter there is a champion although always drunk. Nobody else has the smallest chance of getting anything till we have finished. We get as far as the depot but the infernal skunk of a baggage man refuses to check our things so we refuse to go and after the train goes there is a free fight which culminates in our arrest. The skunks are about 10 to 1 but produce pistols and shout for police. On our arrival at the cooler the man can think of no charge to bring except insult and eventually withdraws it altogether so we are discharged and after divers drinks, adjourn to Basin Street where Reginald and I pass the night very comfortably with NY Minnie and Lou. The Doc very drunk faces Mrs. Stanley but does not stay.

Account of our trouble with the baggage man at N.O.
Jan 17th, 85.
Having previously obtained tickets to Jax [Jacksonville] Pemberton, Reginald, Doc and I arrived at L and H depot quite half an hour before time. Fred and Cap walked up to see us off. The fellow who was checking the baggage first objected to two boxes saying there was no place to fasten a check to. After that, he said they did not contain wearing apparel. On being told they did he said, "Oh John Bull is not going to have his own way here." and "We do things different to what they do in your country." I said, "You are certainly a very long way behind us." and Fred, "They have a little more sense over there."

He was furious at this and declined to check any of our things at all till the train was moving off. He then got a lot of blacks and people round him evidently expecting a row. Reginald went up to him and said you damned son of a b[itch] what do you mean by making us miss the train? He then struck at Reginald and just touched him in the face and all the blacks crowded round and one fellow, who I would swear was a policeman, struck at Reginald's head with a heavy stick but luckily only caught him on the arm. A darkie was squaring round very pluckily when Fred just stepped in front of him and he immediately fled. Meanwhile, one of the fellow's pals produced a pistol and was going to shoot Reginald when Fred spotted him and said, "You coward." and he put it up.

Meanwhile, the police had come up in force and the skunk of a baggage man kept shouting "Arrest that man!" and Reginald was marched off to the cooler. I went with him leaving the Doc to look after the dogs etc. On our arrival at the station, Reginald was searched and the head man told him [he] had better settle the matter if possible as it being Saturday night he would have to be locked up till Monday. The prosecutor then came in as white as a sheet and mumbling all over and when asked what the charge was could find nothing to say at first. He eventually stammered out, "This gentleman called me a _____." The charge was then entered as insult. Hardly had he left the room when he returned and said in a shaky voice, "I would like to withdraw the charge against this gentleman." And then [he] returned. Presently, Fred came in with the inspector and after some handshaking all round we all walked out together parting the best of friends.

It seems curious that anyone can be arrested and carried off and searched just because any common blackguard shouts out arrest and also Americans being such great people for traveling put up with the treatment they receive from all railway officials and especially baggage men.

The Cap was described as Archer's private secretary in the Hot Springs paper and in one of the N.O. dailies as a "Noted London Sport."

[The following section is a newspaper article from the New Orleans Times Democrat. *Copied by Evelyn Booth.]*
Jan 18, 85.
N.O.
"It has been reserved for New Orleans to furnish Archer something to think about besides himself. It seems that he and his friends went to the L and H Depot last evening intending to take the cars for a fashionable Florida winter resort, and having some difficulty about their baggage and being talked to the way peculiar to trunk handlers and the train meanwhile moving off, resented it and blows were exchanged. One round was fought bare knuckles go as you please in which it is said the jockey and his friends had the best of it. The party missed their train and intend leaving for the west today on a great hunt."

[The following is a corroboration written by John Frizzle.]
Sunday
January 11th 85.
Came home about 11 o'clock after having a very hard night, missed Evelyn some way and had breakfast by self. Fred Archer appeared and we went on [a] Tram to [the] Exposition saw no one there that we knew. Looked at horses left on [the] way back interested quack doctor who was selling medicine. Went to Trinity Church[37] but too soon and did not stay long (Fred Archer's birthday).

Example of Native American performers in Buffalo Bill's Wild West
DENVER PUBLIC LIBRARY

Monday
January 12th 1885
Started off in [a] cab with Fred Archer to pick up Evelyn at the celebrated
Mrs. Stanley's failed to find him there so went to Station and found John-
son waiting for us. Arrived in time for train got dogs and guns in.

Tuesday
January 13th 1885
Fine morning got up rather late very tired after shooting the day before.
[I] went round with Evelyn and Pemberton to have breakfast.

Wednesday
14th January 85.
Dull wet morning up by 9 o'clock after breakfast went all of us to get
photographed. Fred Archer, Evelyn, Reginald and myself brought dogs

with us and guns had a great time of it. Arrived back about 1.30 saw the great Pemberton.

Sunday
January 18th, 85
New Orleans
Packing the order of the day get through about 3 o'clock p.m. went over with Fred Archer to say goodbye to Bush and Johnson saw the latter and had a bottle of yellow label which was very good indeed. [We] started [out] at 8 o'clock that evening for Jacksonville. People at [the] station did not say very much after the night before. Left [the] Cap behind. I was not sorry.

Monday
January 19th 85
On our way to Jacksonville; [the] journey [was] a rough one and the way anything but interesting however, we pass the time playing cards and eating LL. Have state room, as they call it, and can do just as we like but those whose olfactory nerves are caustic could never miss the good old smell of H2S. Sorry to say, Fred is given the way. Arrived at our journeys end at 1 o'clock at night three hours late came to St. James Hotel and had a good drink.

Tuesday
January 20th 85
Had breakfast at 10.30 Fred Archer and myself out to inspect the celebrated town of Jacksonville; lots of orange trees but did not see the wonderful groves that one hears so much about. After a brisk walk round the town, [we] landed into a first class sporting house; the girls anything but good looking. Not asked to stand a drink so said we would call again in the evening. Reginald and Evelyn go and recover game bag. All meet again at lunch, nothing particular till 7 o'clock dancing the order of the evening. I must say that it's damn bad. Fred meets Chicago gentleman and we go and have drinks "galore." Forgot to say at 5 o'clock went off with Reginald to see Mrs. Herb[38] and her girls but Reginald had no desire

to stay so we landed back to the hotel. Had [a] telegram from Captain Bowling saying he had started from New Orleans. Go to bed early Fred comes in and tells us he's not drunk but [is] very full. Reginald in next room gives out they pay in a very thick matter. Try to find Clinton but fail.

Wednesday
January 21st 85
[This entry is blank.]

CHAPTER FIVE

Hunting and Fishing in Florida

[The following is written by Evelyn Booth.]
Jan 18. 85.
Have a long talk with [an] agent of L and N Railway[1] who is very civil
and promises a thorough inquiry into the baggage man's conduct. Succeed in getting off at fast leaving Cap behind. The train goes through Alabama, West Florida, [and] Georgia and then into Florida again through
the usual uninteresting sort of country and we reach Jax at 1 a.m. Go to
St. James Hotel[2] and succeed in getting a drink. Fred sleeps with the Doc.

In the morning, we explore the town but don't think much of it.
Beastly cold day raining hard. Find the St. John's[3] boat leaves [the] next
day and decide on making a start. Doc and Fred find out bawdy house
but the fowl are inferior. [We] find [an] English ready money bookie on
their return and drink with him. There is a ball here every night but the
women are a dowdy set.

Jan 21. 85.
Leave Tocoi[4] landing in Chesapeake at 2.30 and proceed up [the] St. John
River which here is very wide. Find too late there is no liquor on board
and make a rush at Palatka[5] where we stop after supper and get beer and
whisky. Sleep fairly well in spite of the noise made by Fred and Doc next
door and after breakfast in the morning find we have arrived at Sanford[6]
the highest point the Chesapeake goes to. Make up our minds to get on
at once as the little steamer is alongside and ready to start. [We] part from
Fred here [and] he is rather low at leaving us. After [a] farewell drink, we
get our traps and ourselves on the Astatula[7] and after a long delay cross

Lake Monroe[8] and go up the upper St. John which is very narrow and winding. Any amount of poldoos and white and blue cranes and a good many teal and ducks. The Astatula is crammed and we can get no cabin to ourselves and the food is wretched. Try trolling but meet with no success. We pass a pretty little place with [a] fair orange grove. It is occupied by a Northerner who gave $10,000 dollars for it. The steward makes up some shake downs in the cabin and seven of us sleep there. It is frightfully hot owing to the steam pipes. Get up early and try trolling again with better luck catching altogether seven black bass, [the] biggest [is] seven pounds.

There are generally a lot of gators and moccasins to be seen from the boat but it is a cold wet day and very few show themselves. Arrive at Rockledge[9] landing just as it gets dark and what a place. A platform standing in the water and some wagons with mules up to their bellies in the water. We load up two wagons and drive through the water to Rockledge about three miles arriving at the Tropical House[10] in about 1 ½ hours. It is nicely situated on a bank above the Indian River[11] and surrounded by orange trees loaded with fruit. Get a good supper which we want badly and inspect a boat which looks as if it would suit our purpose and the proprietor is a German and as civil as possible. He knows the coast well and has been as far as Key West. He recommends [to] us the inlet for sport.

Jan 24, 85.
Make a start for Titusville[12] north of Rockledge after dinner leaving the dogs behind. Eileen is very near her time now.[13] Kill a good many ducks on the way but they are raft ducks[14] a breed new to us and not much good. There is a clinking breeze and we run up well reaching Titusville 20 miles in time for supper. Find there is no whisky to be got and that we shall have to go to Oak Hill[15] at the head of the river for it. The head of the river is a great place for gators. By the way, this is not a river at all but a narrow salt water lagoon and shallow in most places. There are thousands of poldoos round Titusville and quite tame. The hotel there where we stayed for the night is bad and very expensive. In the morning, run up to the head of the river and dispatch John (our cook and the baldest colored fellow on record) to Oak Hill for whisky. While he is gone Reginald and the Doc land and beat the marsh but only produce two snipe and a raft

duck. John returns about 6 p.m. with a load of beer but only 1 gallon of whisky. We have the tent on deck and intend sleeping there but it comes on to blow hard about dark with heavy rain squalls and it looks odds on it being blown away but it hold[s] on all night though we pass an uncomfortable night.

In the morning, Reginald and John depart in search of alligators but fail to see [any] and it being too cold and stormy. On their return, make tracks for Titusville again stopping to look at Jackson's grove on the way. It has come on to blow stiff and two boats, which have come through the handover, funk the crossing. One contains a fat man who calls himself a commodore. On our arrival at Titusville, we have to get a new rudder which takes all day to make and the unhappy poldoos suffer heavily in consequence. Stop at Titus again for the night. It has turned quite cold and there are no bedclothes. In the morning, make tracks for Rockledge which we reach in the evening having been becalmed for a long time and when we did get a wind it was right ahead. The dogs were delighted to see us. Eileen [has] not pupped yet. Spend evening till supper inspecting orange groves which seem to be all for sale.

Jan 28, 85.
Leave Rockledge after breakfast for St. Sebastian, 48 miles.[16] Lovely day and a good breeze. Get to the mouth of the creek at 3 p.m. having killed nothing on the way. Get up the first mile with a good breeze. It is straight here but it soon begins to wind. We come round a bend onto a huge gator but he is too quick for a 50 Winchester bullet. This is the only gator we see before reaching a good camping place where there is no hammock to get through the water. We determine to sleep on the boat but have supper on shore and sit before [a] rousing fire for some time afterwards, and hear some blood curdling tales about rattlers from John.

Get up at 5 a.m. and Paul,[17] Doc and I start for the fishing ground leaving Reginald and John to bring up the dingy with tent etc. See plenty of deer sign on the way and 3 lots of quail. After about 3 miles, come to large open prairie. Kill [a] sea eagle[18] which the Dr. spends an hour skinning. On Reginald's arrival with the pole he begins to catch bass quick, some of them 5 lbs. [and] give good sport. They only lie in dead water and take yellow fly freely. The buzzards have a *mauvais quart d'hair*.[19] Get back to camp where Doc kills a lovely parakeet, queen body, gold and crimson head. Find bass is first class eating and that John is a superior baker. It comes on to pour about dark and continues all night but does not bother as much.

Jan. 30 85.

Rain clears off after breakfast and we start for the bird roost about 3 miles up the creek. On the way, kill a good many bass but no large ones. See some very fresh deer sign. On arriving at the roost, find any amount of fowl but no egrets.[20] Kill white crane, ibis,[21] water turkey[22] and some more eagles. On the way back to camp kill at least 20 bass and bream out of one small hole but large ones are not on the job today. Very rough going along the creek and we all get back wet to the skin. Determine to get back to the ship as the sky looks very threatening and leave after dinner. It pours all the way. The boat division make good time arriving soon after us. Have seen several gators but got no shots as they are very wide awake. To bed early after hot whisky, another wet night.

It rained all the night [through] and no one felt too well so we left after breakfast for the main river. Saw only one gator on the way down and shot at him but no result. Splendid day for getting our things dry. Stop at a store below St. Sebastian to lay in supplies and get some oysters but they are no good as the water is not salt enough. Soon reach the narrows and go on through them till it got dark and lulled us to sleep beautifully.

Feb 1 85.

Lovely morning. Make start for the inlet early and get there in about two hours catching a sea trout on the way. Strong current running when we get near and we leave the big boat and walk across about 50 yds to the ocean beach. The remains of a steamer wrecked some years ago stick up out of the sand. There are signs of rabbits but no holes. Any number of shells of all sorts lying about. Start fishing for sharks but none appear. A small schooner comes in as far as the bar and sends two boats to shoot a net inside. They have a rough time coming through the breakers and a worse one going back being apparently heavily loaded with fish. It is unlawful to come and take fish from one stall to another but they would take a lot of catching here as the sheriff is at Titusville. These fishing schooners take their load on ice to Savannah or Charleston.[23] Another party are camped on the point. They have caught very little and lost all their hooks to sharks and altogether seem mugs. Two of them are very old. One of them has a small orange grove at the head of the river.

Reginald and Paul go across to the other side and see plenty of sharks. John funks the crossing saying he is not going to risk his life in a flat bottomed boat where there are sharks. There is no water of any good to be got here and the sand flies are a curse after sundown so we get back to the boat as quick as possible and try to get rid of the brutes by smoke and lemons etc. No fish to be caught at this place at all and we could not stand the flies long enough to wait for the tide coming up. One shark came at my bait but the hook did not hold him. On getting back to the sea gull pole, up till we get to open water and after supper have a great concert fiddle, banjo and concertina all playing in different keys and time. John says Frizzle is the hardest doctor he has ever met.

Another lovely day to go to the west side of the river for water etc. old chap called Russell lives here, supposed to be a great hunter. [The] ruins of Fort Capron[24] [are] still [a] remaining relic of Seminole war. Reginald and Frizzle go and breakfast at Russell's. He sticks them for 75 cents each and gives them nothing to eat. However, he guarantees deer, no deer no pay. Which sounds fair enough. He then departs to search for horses but fails to find any so the hunt has to be postponed. Go down with Paul in [a] small boat to store about 3 miles off [and] find it shut up and no one about. Take a long time getting back against strong wind. Find out [a] good place for snapper fishing. Paul [is] in high spirits as [there is] news of [a] dance near, he changes his clothes and rushes off immediately on our return. It must be poor fun as there are hardly any women and no refreshments. Lay in supply of limes which are delicious.

Reginald departs early with Russell after deer and the Doc goes off in another direction with one of his boys, a youngster of about 8. Paul, who is very cheap after the night, and John go off in [a] dingy to catch bait but are not successful. However, we are too late at the inlet as the tide is running out like a mill race and we catch nothing but cats. The good fish only bite while the tide is running in which for some accursed reason is only about two hours out of twelve. Saw a great many sharks of all sizes some very large ones on the bar but though several took the bait none fastened. Had one or two good bass on but Ryder's[25] wretched hooks broke at the smallest struggle. Of course as I had no gun, the cranes, egrets, etc. to say nothing of the sharks, swarmed round the boat. I certainly could have killed six of the latter within five yards of the boat. To add to our discomfiture the wind dropped altogether and we had to anchor and wait at the mercy of the sand flies for four hours till the tide turned. We eventually got to the Sea Gull at 10 p.m. and found the Doc asleep. Wake him up and he gives out the crack about a black and white deer which goes into a cave and a lot of other fables, and chaffs Paul about Miss Bell.[26] He talks of going after [her] early next morning. Mrs. Russell is mad at the Doc for keeping one of her brats away all day. Luckily we got a good feed of oysters at the inlet so [we] did not starve.

When John was working on a coasting steamer he one night discovered some water leaking out of a long box and finding it was cold he and his pals proceeded to catch and drink it. In the morning, they were horrified at hearing the mate order someone to "Move that corpse." John said it tasted rather bitter but thought it was owing to the new wood.

At Eden, Richards was one evening giving Captain Miller a flowery account of pineapple growing etc. when the old woman happened to hear some of it and got up and said, "Thomas Richards[27] you are nothing but a big gasbag," and shied a pack of cards at his head.

Feb 4. 85.
Indian River Florida
All up early. The Doc departed with his guide, and Paul and I after catching some fine mullet for bait, with the cast net again, face the inlet. Found the tide just right and began catching fish at once. [There are] red snapper, mangrove snapper,[28] sheepshead[29] and Jew Fish.[30] Had the 8 bore along and of course never saw a shark and no cranes in shot. Killed a pelican about 90 yards [off] could of killed any number of fish if we had, had good hooks but all the fish were large and kept breaking us every minute.

Sheepshead are [the] most comical brutes with teeth just like sheep and average about 8 lbs. Shot some ducks on the way back and delighted John with the fish. Heard the "old Sharp" going off repeatedly. Just got back in time to escape heavy rain storm quite cooler today. The Doc returned shortly with some snipe and quail but had seen no deer. He brought also the feet of a large eagle. The Hon. Cody[31] returned with old Russell soon after. They had seen several deer but got no shot and finished up with a coon hunt reported highly exciting. Cody had nothing to eat while away and made up the deficiency with great rapidity. Old Russell gave him a long account of the Civil War.

Started off with Cody for the inlet sport came as usual and hooks rather rottener, if possible. Had heavy shooting at gulls and pelicans [all] about saw no sharks. On our way back met party who came with us on Astatula. They were in [the] wrong place and caught nothing. Their sharp anchored close to us and we interviewed their Doc and got whisky from him. Quite a treat. Our Doc picked up an old human bone and was greatly delighted. Won a quarter from old Russell betting about weight of 8 bore guns. Russell might have a good orange grove but he gives it no care and the trees are nearly all soar [sic]. Came on rough at dark and wet night.

Feb. 6, 85.
John appeared with news of explosions in London. Houses of parliament and "White Tower" blown up and Rossa[32] sent to England in irons. Reginald landed and found report in paper partially correct. White Tower was the Tower of London nothing about Rossa. Get off after this and stopped at Fort Pierce[33] the last decent store on the way down. Laid in supplies and left for Eden about noon arriving there in time for supper. Find small hotel kept by "Capt" Richards (no one here is under the rank of captain). His daughter is a fine fowl. There is also a niece. Some old fellows from the North stay here every winter for their health. The Captain relies on pineapples for making his fortune. According to figures they even beat oranges. Wonder where drawback comes in. They have all got their knife into our friend Ryder. It seems he has been warning people against coming down here. Retire to sleep on the boat and have another concert discord worse than ever.

Example of Florida's landscape DENVER PUBLIC LIBRARY

Eden, Fla.

After breakfast had [a] long talk with [a] sportsman from Kansas City he has been down here regularly for some years. He has [a] Kennedy Rifle[34] very much like [a] Winchester with Lyman and cracks it up tremendously. Then went and fished for bass in the savannah behind Richard's house. He said it beat St. Sebastian into fits but the result after a patient wait trial with fly and spinner was a small bream about 2 oz. weight and not a sign of a bass. Retired and shot poldoos with the Doc. Richards and the Methuselah's left for Indian River inlet in the middle of the day so we were left to take care of the fowl. [I] had another try for bass in the evening with the same result. Richard's son is building a boat flat bottomed. He says it is worth a $100 dollar bill when finished and seems dirt cheap. [I] had long talk with young chap from the Bahamas. He was very enthusiastic about the culture of pineapples. According to his figures they pay $6,000 dollars per acre but he guesses a good deal and is not reliable.

Feb 8, 85.

Left Eden after breakfast for Jupiter Narrows.[35] Found Peter Wright[36] had arrived [in] the night with "Lord and Lady Stuart" on board. The "Lord" turned out to be Villers Stuart[37] from Waterford. They had some fair fishing at Jupiter Inlet, and [had] seen either a panther or a bear between Lake Worth[38] and the inlet!!! They departed before us northward. Had head wind all the way to the narrows and saw nothing of interest. Reginald had defeated John at poker two days ago and gave him his revenge at "Prick the Garter,"[39] 3 Card Monte, and "Skin."[40] John was completely defeated at each and all and swore he would never play cards again. Stopped for [the] night at head of [the] narrows and rowed across with Doc to ocean beach. There were some fine rollers coming in. Saw no game of any description the Doc and John told ghost stories nearly all night.

Bad wind again this morning and we had to stop after going about two miles. Saw first manatee. Large steamer passed close in shore going south. Left for shore in dingy and caught good sea trout on the way the Doc discovered a large snake immediately on landing which was slain by the "old Sharp" after [an] exciting chase. It was black in color and about seven feet long. Loafed about on the beach and picked up cocoanuts, sea beans, etc. till evening. Found mosquitoes very bad and poled on as far as Peck's Lake[41] where we stayed for the night.

Feb. 10, 85.

Wind more favorable this morning after [a] rough night. [We] got off early and poled through a very narrow channel for some distance running aground every few yards. Eventually the channel got wider and we were able to hoist the jib and make some headway. Got out the trolling lines on arriving at Hope Sound[42] and caught cavalla[43] as fast as we could haul them in. They pulled hard for a little but gave in quick. Caught 19 altogether, three of them about ten pounds. Soon after leaving Hope Sound came to Jupiter light. The keepers houses are quite picturesque. Anchored close to old hulk "Steadfast" which used to be a U.S. survey ship and is now a kind of hotel. The man in charge is a Northerner and very civil. Had hasty lunch and went down to look at the bar which did not look formidable. Saw any number of sharks swimming slowly about and sent the Doc back after rifles and hooks. During his absence, put charge of no. 5 shot into one's head at a distance of three yards. They would not take our bait so went for a walk on the beach. Saw remains of three wrecks. Any amount of lovely shells of all sorts. Had supper on "Steadfast" for a change and had long talk with a Brooklyn man who is staying here for a few days. He is a Republican and proud of it. The first one we have met since the election. Sat up talking till a late hour for us now.

It came on to blow fresh in the night and is comparatively cold this morning. Went down first thing [in the morning] to have a look at the shark line and found [the] bait gone. Four masted steamer passed very close in here to keep out of the gulf stream but it looks a very risky proceeding. Another steamer passed soon after and a sailing ship all going south. The professors arrived about midday and brought some papers but very old. They had killed two deer in St. Lucie[44] which made old Russell mad. Went for a long walk along the shore with the Doc and got a great variety of shells and saw some fresh bear tracks. Cody went trolling and caught several cavalla and succeeded in smashing his rod and losing his bait at the finish. The wind still continued so we put the tent up on the shore. Had a long talk with Martin (the professor's boatman) about war and oranges. He was a Union man and got hit at Petersburg.[45] Read Sherman's memoirs[46] mostly, leaving on the same subject (the war).

Feb. 12, 85.
Jupiter
Up early. Slight rain and still heavy wind. Went to look for a deer and saw great many tracks some very fresh. Walked right on top of one lying down but [the] scrub [was] so thick [I] could not shoot. Returned and found Cody and the professors had caught sixty cavalla and blue fish. After dinner, dived for them again but were not so successful. It came on to rain heavy and the tent was full of frogs and lizards etc.

Feb 13, 85.
Rained in torrents nearly all night, but tent stood it well. Started to look for deer again after breakfast. All the old tracks had been washed out

and did not discover a fresh one for a long time. Just then a heavy thunderstorm came on and drenched us. Went shark shooting after dinner. Everything so wet determined to stay on hulk for the night and found it terribly hot.

Feb 14.

Wind being fair made up our minds to start northward. The man on [the] *Steadfast* takes the cake for extortionate charges. Made flourishing start and got on well for a short distance when Paul got in a terrible funk about an imaginary squall and anchored. He is a wretched sailor and would die in a real storm. [We] caught any amount of cavalla and occasional trout and bass. Came on to rain again as usual and the wind chopped round to the north causing [us] to anchor at the head of the narrows which made us all very cross.

Feb. 15, 85.

Made an early start and made slow progress for 3 hours but a heavy rain squall came up from the south and brought us up to Eden flying. Found same party there still with the exception of Kansas City man and also two Canadians. It continued very wet all day and nothing was done. Found papers with [the] account of London explosions and Stewart's Battle and the fall of Khartoum.[47] All the people here in excitement about [a] wreck on ocean beach just opposite. Steamer loaded with sugar and cigars and not insured. It seems she sprang a leak at sea and the cap succeeded in running over on shore without loss of life. The Captain was part owner and had just spent $9,000 dollars in repairs and this was the first trip she had taken without being insured. Any amount of cigars to be had for the asking. [I] had [a] long talk with [a] young fellow who lives in a tent below Richards. He is very delicate and the damp climate does not suit him at all and he talks of leaving shortly. A terrible wet night.

Weather still bad. The Doc and Paul went off with a young chap, called Dixon, to the wreck. Spent the day loafing around Eden. After supper we were sitting in the verandah when up came the Doc with a quart bottle of rum under one arm a lager beer bottle full under the other an 8 bore gun in one hand and a canvas bag full of cigars and cigarettes in the other. The bottle was immediately passed around. The Bahaman fellow got a good suck and sham round for five minutes. An old German called Deshler was also on a fair way to get full. With great difficulty we succeeded in dissuading the Doc from going into the house and brought him out to the boat. We had seen no sign of Paul, and the Doc could only say, "Paul's paralytic." On our way out we passed Dixon's boat and saw a curious looking object hanging over the side. This on investigation turned out to be Paul perfectly speechless and very sick. Reginald and John went and put him safe inside and then Reginald went ashore. He returned later about 1 a.m. having found his room occupied and reported Paul was still throwing up his inside. Meanwhile, the Doc had escaped and came back very wet having fallen off the pier. He then went to bed and quickly fell twice off the cabin top so he retired inside and the subsequent proceedings interested him no more.

Tent fell on us about 5 a.m. and got us out early. Had coffee and started for the wreck. Paul could be smealt [sic] 5 miles off. Went up to trail across to [the] beach where the Doc, who was very cheap, decided to remain for the day. Could see only a small bit of steamer which had broken up fast, went down to [the] beach about 3 miles to where the flags were flying passing on the way a good deal of promiscuous wreckage. Found the men round a fire with not a whole suit of clothes among them. Asked for the Captain and found him sitting in a tent. Had a drink of real Dublin Stout and a talk on politics when Richards and Co. came up. The Captain was taking things very coolly and was as nice a fellow as I have ever met.

Held an auction and disposed of diver's articles at varying prices. John became the proprietor of some red plush cushions and Paul of some canvas and a clock. Richards deliberately started knocking out some bolts under [the] Captain's eyes and evidently hoped to get everything for nothing. Said farewell to Captain who hoped to be able to come up with us and went back to the boat and found the Doc recovered but he had been torpid enough to allow someone to sneak a bottle of rum from the little boat.

Feb. 18, 85.
Found [the] boat had arrived during the night with two young Boston fellows on board names Belmont[48] and Mygatt.[49] They have a red and white

setter and dachshund with them. They are at Harvard and supposed to be there now so I should imagine [they] have an easy time there. Young Belmont started with the avowed intention of making us fight on rye whisky and succeeded in getting beautifully drunk himself. Went out with him in rowboat and he had marvelous escapes from falling overboard. The Captain of the *America*,[50] Miller, and his mate Colson,[51] arrived with Richards having sold him the wreck for $125 dollars!!! Belmont and Reginald attacked the whisky again after supper and the former finished by puking in the verandah.

Intended starting north but the wind was what Paul called a "Blue Norther" and he said it was impossible to go. Belmont and Co. departed south after dinner. On receiving their bill they were surprised to find $1 dollar a day charged for their board and an extra item of 1 ½ dollar for being sick! This fairly takes the Abernethy.[52] Spent the evening at card tricks and had Cap Miller successfully at pricking the garter. He has loaded us with Havana cigars and absolutely the best cigarettes on record. Every snake in the county seemed to be on foot today and we saw four different kinds in as many minutes.

Belmont captured a possum in the morning, a spiteful cuss. Wind still bad but left Eden about noon after prolonged leave talking with everybody gave them a royal salute at parting. Found six on board made a tightish fit. The Cap chaffed Paul unmercifully about his double reefed sails and the unsailor like appearance of his rigging. Got up to Fort Pierce[53] about dark and anchored for the night. Had great concert wind up and the Doc and John danced.

Still same Norther and our progress was painfully slow. Saw strange steamer engaged in getting oysters. Got up to the narrows about 4 p.m. and found current so strong could make no progress at all. Reginald, Doc, and the Cap went on shore for a shoot and killed several varieties of cranes etc. After supper, had great debate about marriage and such matters and Reginald horrified the Cap by his advanced ideas about women.

Feb. 22, 85.
Wind dropped during the night but still kept foul. The oyster steamer came up and passed us and very nearly ran us down on Paul meanly

refusing to give them information about the channel. My opinion is he knows nothing about it himself. Made a start poling after breakfast. Supplies are beginning to run short as we did not reckon on being a week on the journey. Stayed for the night at a palmetto hut where two fellows from Chicago live. They are cultivating tomatoes. Had a hot supper, quite a treat, Paul was not quite so sulky after a good gorge.

Feb. 23, 85.
Started against head wind and made slow progress as far as New Haven where we succeeded in buying out the whole store with two dollars our whole remaining capital.[54] About 3 p.m. the wind shifted to the east a little and we were at last able to make some headway and arrived at Rockledge at 10 p.m. Found Bevan[55] who had left his boat in disgust and come up that day on the oyster steamer. He joined us in a hearty vote to censure on the Indian River boatmen. Doc and self came on shore but Reginald and the Cap and Colson stayed on the boat. There are a good many people staying at Ryder's and he has all the best of the pickings on this river. Richards has about as much chance of snowfall in Hell. Killed a good many ducks on the way up but luckily got to R and L before we needed to use them. Oranges seemed better than ever and a bed was quite a luxury as we had not used one for a month. Poor Eileen died soon after we left and the Dr. here examined her and found three dead pups. Of course the other brutes are all right.

Feb. 24, 85.
R. L. Fla.
Spent the morning inspecting orange groves and sampling the produce of each Capt. Miller has the orange fever bad. Colson made the best record at eating -32-. Bevan left in the middle of the day for the St. Augustine[56] after giving us a pressing invitation to visit him there. Quite the nicest American we have met but he has spent most of his life on the other side. Went and weighed in the store and found Reginald and I had increased and the Doc lost on the trip. A sportsman staying here went over to Merritt's Island[57] and killed 15 snipe in a short time so there must be some shooting to be got there. They are all utterly ignorant about birds and

call redshank oyster catchers, stint, etc. all snipe. Reginald and the Cap went up to a place which is for sale about 1 ½ miles up the river but did not report favorably. The republican we met at Jupiter is on his way to St. Augustine via Daytona and New Smyrna[58] and the Cap and Colson are going to avail themselves of his offer of a passage. We are all sorry at having to part. All went for a poach after oranges at 11 p.m. to load their boat with.

The Cap and Colson left directly after breakfast which we had together at [a] restaurant. The Doc had made an early start for Merritt's Island. Reginald and I spent the morning inspecting more groves with young Magruder.[59] "Old Man Magruder" is away at New Orleans. The Doc and Co. returned before us with 14 couple of snipe. A fellow called Wilkinson,[60] the son of [the man] whose house was burnt, was very anxious to buy the black dog and offered draft on Richmond, VA for $125 dollars in payment. Mrs. Ryder, who was watching, gave us the tip that he was no good so the deal came to nothing. He seemed about half drunk and we heard that he had found some pure <u>alcohol</u> which the Dr. had inadvertently left out and [he] polished it off. He promised us some splendid quail shooting in his orange grove!!!! Had great trouble with John over his accounts which were slightly confused. Out of $80 dollars received he could only produce a bill for $29 and yet confidently pointed out an entry in his book "Due to John Sawyer" $9 dollars and seemed greatly injured on being told that did not quite correspond. Reginald eventually packed him off with a flea in his ear. Made fresh acquaintance in [the] evening with Captain May[61] a confederate who was in Stuart's Cavalry[62] and took part in 350 different engagements. He seemed to think the old country was in a very bad way but said he would be over fighting for us in Egypt[63] if he had not a family to take care of. He ridiculed the idea of Northerners getting hold of his whole place and said that all the best groves on the river were in the hands of Southerners who meant to keep them.

Ryder and a large party made an early start to look at some of the possessions on the island and Reginald announced his intention of having a go for the Mrs. but was afraid Parker might cut him out. However, May appeared with his rowboat and Reginald on seeing a flask of whisky in the boat thought he would earn some by rowing up with him. A big load came in from the Astatula all very sick after the journey but most of them very anxious to go down the river and see the narrows etc. If they had our experience of them they might not be quite so eager. Spent the day talking to new arrivals and loafing around with the Doc eating oranges and putting big spiders into nests. The spiders soon succumbed and apparently made no fight at all. Went to bathe down the river a bit but funked at the sight of a moccasin which slipped into the water at the very spot we had selected. Had the old argument over again about the free country.

CHAPTER SIX

Shootout with Bill and the Journey Home

Feb. 27, 85.

Started early with the Doc for the island and soon get to the snipey place. Found it good going and very good lying ground but not many snipe and had to shoot very straight to kill 12 couple. Cody came and fetched us in Ryder's boat and wore a very satisfied air, he referred us to his bed for an explanation. This on inspection was a disgusting sight and the Doc, by the aid of a microscope, discovered some animalcula[1] but no longer living. The Doc discovered a pond back in the wood where wood ducks come in thick in the evening. Saw several snakes in the morning and one large gator, shot one of the snakes about four feet long. Doc and I started back to St. Johns prairie after quail but only found two after a long hunt. There was a lot of water about and no sign of game of any description. Spent the afternoon trying to upset Ryder's boat but found it by no means easy to manage at all. In the evening made the acquaintance of a funny little girl born in England but out here for five years, only 15 but quite ready for it. Had a lesson in American slang from her, she informed me that only the bad girls wore their hair frizzed in England and said she knew all about them. The Doc her and her mother [went] out for a row in the evening and [he] crammed them full of fables about Arkansaw etc.

March 1, 85.

Went on [the] snipe interest again and, as neat as a touch, upset going across in a sudden squall. There was a good deal of wind and the snipe were wild and hard to hit. The bag amounted to 7 couple of snipe, a rail bittern and some poldoos. As usual saw a lot of snakes. Get excitement

William Frederick "Buffalo Bill" Cody (1846–1917) was the most famous American during his lifetime. He was an American scout, bison hunter, and showman.

in the evening at the arrival of the Indian River. All the people who were staying at Eden were on board and glad to leave. Hear that the *Zephyr* (Peter Wright's boat) had been blown on shore below Jupiter. Saw the "Dutch Doctors" and Martin on their way north but not near enough to interview them. On the steamer had to wait some time to repair her floats some of which had been smashed on an oyster bar.

Very windy morning. Went out with Reginald in the "Ryder" after ducks and killed a lot but so rough could not pick many of them up. Had great hopes of wrecking the "Ryder" but only succeeded in smashing the foremast and ran her on shore in [a] disabled state. In the afternoon, rowed down to her with the Doc and rigged up the mast in a sort of a way and brought her triumphantly into port. Cultivated the queer little girl more, she said that if a girl had big lips that it was a sure sign of her being fond of kissing. The Doc made [a] strong running [at her]. And [he] spent part of the evening with her in the other Doc's hammock. Great conjuring séance in the evening, there is another "Harvard" (or as they prefer to be called) Cambridge fellow here, a friend of Belmont's. He seems fond of sport but has only just recovered from a severe illness. From his account, they seem to be able to do just what they like there. Belmont and Mygatt have got leave for a month on a doctor's certificate and are supposed to be suffering from consumption!!!! (Of whisky?)

March 3, 85.
Rockledge Fla.
Nothing to be done as there was no wind for sailing and they forgot to call us early to go to the island. Phillips has been here since we were over but failed to produce any snipe. He must be a duffer and it is hard to make out his position here. Have heard from May that Ryder goes busted every year regularly and goes up to New York and gets some goods somehow and lets his creditors trade it off. May is anxious for us to buy a place here as he is unable to fight the "damned Northerners" alone and wants help badly. The little girl departed by Junita [*Waunita*],[2] which is perhaps [just] as well as something would have happened very soon. The conduct of her mother seemed extraordinary. It looked just as if she wanted her to get into trouble. The Doc discovered a couple in the act back in the scrub

but they are not staying here. [There are] several fresh arrivals from the North [here] by way of the haul over. Had talk in the evening with "Ned de Courey."[3] He used to be an actor and step dancer and came down this way for his health. He has had a finger in the smuggling line and says it is good business. He was stopped by a man of war last year and towed back to Key West as he was unable to give a satisfactory account of himself.

Just the same sort of proceedings till Saturday when the Doc and I went to the island intending to burn the high grass in the swamp this we did but the fire spread to the wood and in spite of all we could do burnt all before it for five miles and was then only extinguished by all the inhabitants of Georgiana[4] turning out. Saw very few snipe but killed some parakeets and a turtle. The Doc the day before captured a very large snake of which we preserved the skin.

March 8, 85.

[I] went over with Littauer[5] to the scene of the fire. In the evening a gouger started recitations and psalm singing. The Doc began laughing at him early in the play and he stopped in great indignation. They then retired outside and started rolling the Black Dog up and down the verandah in Mrs. Richards'[6] pram. This failed to stop him so the[y] procured a rotten citron and went round to the back and shied it through the window catching him squarely in the abdomen. I was looking through the window and saw the thing burst all over him. The effect on the women was startling. Some of the old fellows talked a good deal but not one of them had the pluck to do anything. Ryder came in, in a great state and offered $25 dollars reward. "Budd" Wilkinson was there and as he had been very full all day was strongly suspected and was very indignant. He went in to supper and Parker caught him just as he had wolfed a bottle of Worcester, which he said was "prime." The tub thumping did not continue after the citron episode. Some excitement was caused in the afternoon by a nigger shooting at Wilkinson just outside the store but he was full and missed him.

March 9, 85.

Very strong wind blowing went out in the Ryder to the consternation of everybody but got back safe. Letters arrived so at last can leave.

Example of a boxing program from this time period DENVER PUBLIC LIBRARY

March 10, 85.

Ryder had the impudence to ask for money for the use of his rotten boats which however he did not get. Came down upper St. John's in Waunita a vast improvement on Astatula very crowded and had to sleep on deck. Some nice fellows from Kentucky on board, heard just before leaving Rockledge that "old man Wilder" [7] was drowned in the gale yesterday through his boat upsetting.

Left Waunita at Enterprise [8] where we got first rate breakfast and heard news of Alec who has been at Oakhill all the time. Came down St. John's in Steamer *Anita,* [9] fast boat. The stewardess was a bold bad woman and got herself crammed by Cody. Found Jax crowded and could not get in at St. James [hotel] so stayed for the night at Beaver Street. [10] [We] heard several tales about Fred's deeds in the "cat houses." The doc smashed a woman and a bed at one blow, I took on the six footer of the establishment [and] we sampled the whole party at $5 a head.

March 12, 85.

Left Cody in bed and started for New Orleans at 7.30. Very dusty and uncomfortable journey but for a wonder we "made connection" and got in "on time." Got a room at St. Charles [Hotel] and went up to [Cotton] Exhibition which is in very much better condition. Met Crosby from Kansas City had several drinks with him. The man in charge of the life saving station was greatly excited on hearing that we were at [the] wreck of [the] *America* and gave us a great book of reports. [I] had dinner with Bush and Johnson who were very glad to see us back. Called Stanley's in the evening and found Lou and Laura had gone to Montana.

March 14, 85.

Had dinner again at 32 and made the acquaintance of Pat Sheedy who was very civil. Found out several new sporting houses Pat introduced us to a friend of his Yank Adams [11] proprietor of *Chicago Sporting Journal* and a wonder at finger billiards. [I] assisted at a prize fight between Jack Dempsey and Bixamos, [12] a Frenchman 3 stone heavier. It was fought with very small gloves and Bixey was knocked out in five rounds and was cut all to pieces. Dempsey is a nice quiet young fellow and is very anxious to visit the old country.

Some days after this there was another fight between George Fryer,[13] a new arrival from Nottingham, and C Lange[14] of Ohio. They are both fine powerful men and the fight was a good one lasting eleven long rounds when Lange had, had enough. The gloves used were very large which accounted for the long time it lasted.

For several days there had been some talk of a match between Buffalo Bill and I and the day following the Fryer-Lange fight I was formerly introduced to him. An event which has most likely altered the whole of my future proceedings. We four: Cody, Yank, Doc and I went up to his camp to have some shooting and spent a very enjoyable day. Neither of us tried very hard in the shooting and a match was arranged for the following Saturday. While driving back from Oaklands Park who should appear but Belmont and Littaur just from Florida who had seen any account of the proposed match and were on their way to see it. We all had dinner together and had a box at the Grand Opera House.[15] Afterwards during the performance Littaur bet Belmont 25 dollars he would not run across the stage, which he did. Shortly afterwards, a villainous looking lout appeared and said the manager would like to see him. In response to this, he went downstairs and in five minutes as he did not return we sent down to inquire where he was and found he had been arrested. We then started off for the station and him coming out on parole with orders to show up again the next morning at nine. The judge was very severe and fined him 25 dollars so the bet just paid it. He and Miller appeared at the camp afterwards followed by two Italian fellows at Molly Johnson's[16] the night before and kept them ever since. Belmont and the Doc were going to ride among the Cowboys[17] and when Belmont came out in the blue shirt and buckskin breeches they turned tail and fled.

The next day the match came off. It was terribly windy which prevented accurate shooting. I won [by] three birds killing 40 to 37. Bill immediately challenged me again to shoot on the following Wednesday the day appointed for his benefit and another match was arranged. The next item of importance was an introduction to Miss B,[18] a New York actress, by Bill. This led to good results as also did two other ones, one of them in particular a dear little thing.

On the 31st of March we gave a great dinner to all the Cowboys at Madame Eugene's everyone got very full and a considerable amount of glasses were broken. Buck Taylor and I left early as I had to shoot the next day and old Buck was very full. Directly after we left, Belmont jumped through the window and all the hats were smashed by others. They then went out and were accosted by an officer who said they must go to the station. Two friends of Belmont's crossed the street to see what the trouble was about and the police said they must go too. They turned and ran and the police after them shooting like mad but no, New Orleans policeman was ever yet known to hit anyone he fired at so they escaped.

However, Belmont and 6 more were conveyed to the cooler and fined ten dollars each or twenty days in the morning. When they were locked up they sent round a bid to come and get them out. Con[19] who was among those arrested was very indignant and told the policeman afterwards he would piss on him and make him smell like a man. The papers are full of our proceedings and we are known as the gang.

The next day was Buffalo Bill's benefit and there were about 3,000 people there. The return match was shot off with the following result, Bill 47 Self 46, though three were counted to him which he never touched.[20] In the evening we all got very full and I was arrested for giving the Cowboy yell in the streets. However, Capt Reynolds heard I was in and came and got me out by squaring the judge in the morning. I escaped a fine. As it was getting rather hot [and] some of us being arrested every night I determined to accept Bill's invitation to stay up in the camp and did stay there till they left the town. I occupied the same tent as old Buck and found him a splendid fellow and we became great pals. Today after I took up my abode, Major Burke[21] arrived with 30 fresh Indians and most of the old ones left for the nation to look after their places there. Among the new ones were three squaws, two of them quite good looking.

Belmont left about this time after being telegraphed for several times. He certainly is a scorcher, going on a great hunt with him this fall in the Black Hills.[22] He [Buffalo Bill] was perfectly delighted with my rifles and said he had never seen such weapons before. I sent all my guns and rifles up to his place at North Platte, Neb.[23] He is very anxious to take the whole show over to England next spring and I have had several long talks with him about it and am going to make inquiry on the other side. After some trouble, found agent of West India and Pacific steamers who assured me I should be very comfortable on their boats and anything is better than the horrid railway journey to New York.

Bill went to Mobile on the 9th of April and I went with them. We all went in a box car and were not at all uncomfortable though I had a narrow escape of falling through the open door. Before leaving New Orleans I went to the races once and found them as I expected, utter rot. We had a jolly time in Mobile especially among the coon's and were camped in a very pretty place, Frascati Park[24] and lots of people came to visit us. Buck and I put a peg up in front of our tent and nearly died laughing at the people falling over it as they were always stargazing. Said a sorrowful farewell to all the boys on Tuesday night and came back to New Orleans on Wednesday. Found that the Doc had been full the entire time I was away and that the ship would not sail for another week. Pearl and Queenie had gone to Mexico so Miss Emma was nearly deserted.[25]

The first boxing match on record between Indians took place at the Wild West camp shortly before the dinner and resulted in one being knocked out. They fought very vicious and in quite novel style. The gloves were soaked in blood before two hours. Bill had them on with the big Pawnee Chief who put himself into ridiculous positions.

When we arrived in Mobile early in the morning Buck was sitting with his legs hanging out of the car and looked especially wild looking as he was not quite awake and the long hair was hanging all over his face. A small coon came along looked for a moment and started off and Buck jumped down after him. I doubt the coon has stopped running yet. Found New Orleans very dull when I returned as all the sports had gone to Memphis races and all my favorite girls had left. After two or three ineffectual trials at Molly Johnson's found a nice girl at 68 Union being introduced there by Capt. Hyatt.[26] Went one Sunday to see a game of baseball and was disgusted it is like our rounders with none of the excitement and the pitcher is allowed to throw as hard as he likes.

Hear from all accounts that Bill has a very fine daughter so shall have a good time I hope.[27] He lost a lot of money down at New Orleans but says he will get it all back in one day at Chicago. He once cleared 21,000 dollars there in one day.[28] While I was away with Bill there came a telegram from Reginald at El Paso. The Doc answered it and received reply that the gentleman had left in a great hurry

About a week afterwards, I received another from Hot Springs. Replied at once and get answer that he was not there so could not make it out. Sent all his baggage to New York and wrote to Hoffman [House]. It seems very curious he has never written all this time. The "Bernard Hall"[29] which we were going to sail on was some days late in coming in and her cargo was also not ready. So, we determined to get in "Floridian"[30] another ship of the same line which was leaving before the other. All this time the Doc had been smelling about [for] Lola and imagined himself very much in love with her and was awfully indignant if anything disparaging was said about any of the family. Buck was very much smitten with Mrs. Purnell[31] and asked her to let him have her. She said in reply, "Would you ask me to sin?" And old Buck roared laughing. His girl Cora left the Park Theatre and joined the ladies baseball club according to all accounts a very foolish thing to do as the manager is a ruffian.[32] I met one of the girls who had left them at 68 Union and she gave me a very bad account of him. Pat Duffy[33] has contracted severe gonorrheal opthalmia[34] [sic] and his appearance is not improved by a pair of huge blue goggles. I suppose he contracted it from "she's good company."

Brought all the luggage down to [the] *Floridian* in the afternoon in the middle of a heavy rain storm but thank goodness there were Englishmen and not Americans [there] and all the things were put out of the wet in a minute. Found the Cap on board he stood me a drink and lent me a waterproof coat. [I] got back to dinner at Moreau's[35] with Judge Walker,[36] C[aptain] Hyatt and the Doc, the latter very full already. To our great relief he departed after the soup. The Judge tells us the whole history of Lola's family. Her father, before becoming Bidwell's[37] jackal, used to be spooney [sic] man of an old casekeeper in Mobile and the mother was a big blonde from the north and one of the attractions of the establishment. However, one fine day Tony bolted with the blonde to New Orleans and

William Levi "Buck" Taylor (1857–1924), who was known as "King of the Cow-boys," was a performer in Buffalo Bill's Wild West for many years.
DENVER PUBLIC LIBRARY

married her. The old casekeeper forgave him at the last and left him all her money but two children turned up and the will was set aside. Came down to the ship about nine and went to bed early.

Got up in good time, could see nothing of Doc and made sure he was left. However, got news from the purser that somebody had come on board paralytic the night before and had to be put to bed so felt relieved. We were ready to start at 7 but had to wait for a tug to pull her head round and made a start about 8 am. Met the "Louisiana" coming up, the scenery on both side[s] extremely monotonous. Got down to the jetties about 2.30 after all the talk about them they are extremely disappointing as there is nothing to be seen at all. Left the pilot outside at 3 and [we] are again in blue water. Found everybody on board very nice and the ship beautifully clean however the less said about the other passengers the better. Old Plimsoll[38] is one apparently doddering. He has a wishy washy looking daughter with him.[39] There is also a little woman who looks like a kitchen maid with four brats and a nurse. All the officers are entered for her. There are ten passengers altogether not counting the brats. Rather a contrast to the 330 we came out with. We have a regular menagerie of live animals on board from pigs to turtles. Heard from the Cap the account of Doc's first appearance which was very amusing. He insisted on giving the Cap the account of the bottle of brandy which he assured him had been 15 days in bottle.

[The following entry is a conversation recorded by Booth.]
"Say old feller am I going with you?"
"How do I know," answered the Cap. "Who the devil are you?"
"Oh I'm Frizzle," says the Doc, "and I have the best girl in New Orleans and I left her in tears so I must go back to her." With this, he jumped into a hack and disappeared.

Could see all the light houses along the Florida Keys quite distinctly on Sunday and the last of America I saw was Cape Florida light about ten on Sunday evening. Jupiter light was the last one actually seen about 3 a.m. on Monday.

Any number of flying fish were visible the first few days but disappeared as we got further north. Found the purser a fine sportsman and succeeded in making him very full on several occasions. The Doc spent nearly all his time in bed as he is usual. Was victim of some multitudinous amours. Old Plimsoll is a constant source of amusement at meal times. He is a nailer at eating with a knife and you would want a basket to [pick] up the H's he drops around.

On Wednesday we had to close the ports for the first time, and the ship commenced to roll a little during the night and gradually increased it all day Thursday. Both the women declined dinner but no one else succumbed. There was a heavy swell but no wind of any consequence and still the same warm weather. I spend all my time with the officers as with the exception of an old Scotchman who is a nice old fellow all the others are unmitigated asses.

The swell began to go down on Friday morning and shuffle board etc. were again in vogue. Daily runs only average about 270 miles. They could go faster if they liked but are saving coal. As we got north it begins to get colder but still continues fine. The conversation at dinner time is of the very feeblest description. Down at our end where the officers sit it occasionally gets racy. The Doc stays in bed all day and nurses his afflicted parts. The weather still keeps beautiful and looks like continuing so. The fellow with the red beard and the fellow with the sore lip have great arguments at meal times generally ending in violent personal abuse.

Yesterday evening locked "Waggle"[40] in the WC and kept him there about ½ an hour he was very savage on being released and kept his own room the rest of the evening. Had a conjuring séance in the 2nd officer's cabin afterwards. Have only seen about six vessels all the way but one sailing ship. Some Mother Carey's chickens have attended us all the way so far. Today is the 2,000 wish I was there. Ellen and Button[41] had a slight difference last night about pot of Vaseline which at the finish was pretty evenly distributed over them both.

"Points on America"

Among the advantages of the United States, which every American I have ever met never ceased to praise, the first you come across is the system of expressing and checking baggage. It sounds beautiful in theory but an example of what really happens is as follows:

American Exposition program, Buffalo Bill at the suggestion of many distinguished Englishmen, like Evelyn Booth, took his Wild West show overseas in 1887 to Europe and found great success there.

You arrive at a kind of shed called by courtesy a "depot" and if by good luck you can get anyone to help you with your things you bring them before the dreaded baggage man who begins as follows. "I can't check this because it is not locked or this because it has no handle or this because it does not contain wearing apparel." If you remonstrate you have no chance but by the use of plenty of soft soap you sometimes get them check[ed] but that is only the beginning of your trouble. A man comes through the train collecting checks shortly before the end of the journey. The mug unsuspectingly hands his [in] and is exceedingly lucky if he gets his trunks within 24 hours and anyhow will have to pay 50 cents or rather over two shillings for the transferring of each package, however small, from the depot to the hotel often a distance of less than 100 yards.

Should the baggage man prove unrelenting, your things must go express for which the charge is only $5 dollars per hundred pounds. The cars are nearly always suffocatingly [sic] hot and filthy dirty and there are no decent refreshment rooms en route. The places you stop for 20 minutes to eat are generally small wooden huts and there is nothing fit to eat [or] to be got and hardly ever any liquid refreshment except muddy coffee. It is the rarest thing in the world for a train to be punctual, so much for the railroads. The tracks are without any kind of protection and the sleepers just rough logs laid on the ground. Charges at ordinary rates come to about double our first class fare but there is generally a war of rates going on and the general public profit by this. Most of the lines are in the hands of receivers.

Appendix

Inventory of Game Killed
[The following is a list of game killed by the companions while in Arkansas and Houston, TX. The lists compile the type of animal killed and the date the hunt took place.]

Account of game killed by Reginald Beaumont Heygate, Evelyn Booth, J. P. Frizzle on November 29, 1884 in Arkansaw.

November 29:
R Ducks [0]; B.W. Teal [0]; Y. W. T. [0]; Quail [3.]; Rabbits [0]; Turkey [0]; Various [6.]; Owl [1.]; Buzzard [0]; Wood Duck [0]; Squirrel [0]; Snipe [0]; Dottrell [0]

November 30:
R Ducks [2.]; B.W. Teal [0]; Y. W. T. [0]; Quail [13.]; Rabbits [2.]; Turkey [0]; Various [1.]; Owl [1.]; Buzzard [1.]; Wood Duck [0]; Squirrel [1.]; Snipe [0]; Dottrell [0]

December 1:
R Ducks [8.]; B.W. Teal [0]; Y. W. T. [1.]; Quail [9.]; Rabbits [0]; Turkey [0]; Various [1.]; Owl [0]; Buzzard [0]; Wood Duck [5.]; Squirrel [1.]; Snipe [0]; Dottrell [0]

December 2:
R Ducks [19.]; B.W. Teal [0]; Y. W. T. [1.]; Quail [0]; Rabbits [0]; Turkey [0]; Various [1.]; Owl [0]; Buzzard [0]; Wood Duck [6.]; Squirrel [6.]; Snipe [0]; Dottrell [0]

December 3:
R Ducks [15.]; B.W. Teal [0]; Y. W. T. [1.]; Quail [9.]; Rabbits [0]; Turkey [0]; Various [4.]; Owl [0]; Buzzard [0]; Wood Duck [7.]; Squirrel [0]; Snipe [0]; Dottrell [0]

December 4:
R Ducks [3.]; B.W. Teal [0]; Y. W. T. [1.]; Quail [0]; Rabbits [0]; Turkey [0]; Various [1.]; Owl [2.]; Buzzard [0]; Wood Duck [5.]; Squirrel [1.]; Snipe [0]; Dottrell [0]

December 5:
R Ducks [0]; B.W. Teal [0]; Y. W. T. [0]; Quail [12.]; Rabbits [0]; Turkey [0]; Various [0]; Owl [0]; Buzzard [0]; Wood Duck [0]; Squirrel [0]; Snipe [0]; Dottrell [0]

December 6:
R Ducks [8.]; B.W. Teal [0]; Y. W. T. [0]; Quail [0]; Rabbits [0]; Turkey [0]; Various [0]; Owl [0]; Buzzard [0]; Wood Duck [2.]; Squirrel [0]; Snipe [0]; Dottrell [0]

December 7:
R Ducks [0]; B.W. Teal [0]; Y. W. T. [0]; Quail [10.]; Rabbits [0]; Turkey [0]; Various [0]; Owl [0]; Buzzard [1.]; Wood Duck [0]; Squirrel [1.]; Snipe [0]; Dottrell [0]

Game Killed by Reginald Beaumont Heygate, Evelyn Booth, Fred Archer, and Captain Bowling at Houston, Texas.

December 21:
R Ducks [1.]; B.W. Teal [0]; Y. W. T. [0]; Quail [0]; Rabbits [0]; Turkey [0]; Various [3.]; Owl [0]; Buzzard [1.]; Wood Duck [0]; Squirrel [1.]; Snipe [17.]; Dottrell [0]

December 22:
R Ducks [1.]; B.W. Teal [0]; Y. W. T. [0]; Quail [0]; Rabbits [0]; Turkey

[0]; Various [1.]; Owl [0]; Buzzard [0]; Wood Duck [0]; Squirrel [0]; Snipe [39.]; Dottrell [0]

December 23:
R Ducks [5.]; B.W. Teal [0]; Y. W. T. [1.]; Quail [2.]; Rabbits [0]; Turkey [0]; Various [bittern 5.]; Owl [0]; Buzzard [0]; Wood Duck [0]; Squirrel [0]; Snipe [47.]; Dottrell [0]

December 24:
R Ducks [0]; B.W. Teal [0]; Y. W. T. [0]; Quail [0]; Rabbits [0]; Turkey [0]; Various [0]; Owl [0]; Buzzard [0]; Wood Duck [0]; Squirrel [0]; Snipe [20.]; Dottrell [0]

December 25:
R Ducks [16.]; B.W. Teal [0]; Y. W. T. [1.]; Quail [2.]; Rabbits [0]; Turkey [0]; Various [pelicans 2.]; Owl [0]; Buzzard [0]; Wood Duck [0]; Squirrel [0]; Snipe [1.]; Dottrell [0]

December:
R Ducks [7.]; B.W. Teal [0]; Y. W. T. [0]; Quail [0]; Rabbits [0]; Turkey [0]; Various [0]; Owl [0]; Buzzard [0]; Wood Duck [0]; Squirrel [0]; Snipe [1.]; Dottrell [0]

Letter Combinations
[These letter combinations were found on pages 181 and 183 of the journal.]

a i l n p s t u
alnpstiu, anpstuil, apstuiln, astuilnp, atuilnps, anilnpst, alinpstu, apniln-stu, asilnptis, atilnpsu, auilnpst, Stunpail, Stitpanu, Stulpain, Spuntail, Spantuli

a i l n p s t u
ailstupn, alinputs, alinstup

Business Calling Cards and Tickets
[These business calling cards and tickets were found glued on the back inside jacket of the journal.]

G. H. Phippard, 20 Union Place, Liverpool
Mrs. Henry, Early Hours, Dale S., Boston
"Insurance Retreat" Lunch & Sample Room, 189 Broadway, D. Quirk Prop., New York
Admit One. "THAUMA"
Joe H. Richardson, Cuenin, Gunnison, Colorado
Frederick B. Mims
No. 5 West 24th St.
John T. Burgess, Commercial Editor, *American Grocer, and Dry Goods Chronicle*
Mr. John Daily, 39 West 29th Street

Baggage Claim Ticket
[The baggage claim ticket is for the New York City Transfer and Baggage Express Office: U.S. Barge Express. The following numbers and note are written by Reginald Heygate on the front and back of the ticket. This baggage claim ticket was found taped to page 375 of the journal.]

451, 452, 453, 454, 455, 456, 457, 458
[Note]: Think that very likely the pair will acquire a bedroom after lunch. Reginald Heygate [PS] I hope they won't defile the room.

Envelope
[The envelope was found loose inside the back jacket of the journal.]

[Addressed to]: Evelyn Booth at Hot Springs, Arkansas *[Return address]*: L. Contanseau & Co., Shipping and Commission Merchants, 128 Broadway, New York, NY.

Bibliography

Books

Asbury, Herbert. *The French Quarter: An Informal History of the New Orleans Underworld.* New York: Thunder's Mouth Press, 1936.

Baillie-Groham, William Adolph. *Camps in the Rockies.* Self published, 1882.

Barnette, Michael C. *Encyclopedia of Florida Shipwrecks, Volume I: Atlantic Coast,* (Florida: Association of Underwater Explorers, 2010).

Berlage, Gai Ingham. *Women in Baseball: The Forgotten History.* Westport, CT: Greenwood Publishing Group, Inc., 1994.

Berton, Pierre. *Niagara: A History of the Falls.* New York: McClelland and Stewart Inc., 1992.

Blackstone, Sarah J. *The Business of Being Buffalo Bill: Selected Letters of William F. Cody, 1879–1917.* New York: Praeger Publishers, 1988.

Broderick, Robert C. *The Catholic Encyclopedia.* Nashville, TN: Thomas Nelson Inc., 1976.

Brown, Leslie, and Dean Amadon. *Eagles, Hawks and Falcons of the World.* Great Britain: Hamlyn Publishing Group, 1968.

Brown, T. Allston. *A History of the New York Stage: From the First Performance in 1732 to 1901.* New York: Dodd, Mead and Company, 1903.

Burns, Eric. *The Spirits of America: A Social History of Alcohol.* Philadelphia, PA: Temple University Press, 2003.

Berton, Pierre. *Niagara: A History of the Falls.* New York: McClelland and Stewart Inc., 1992.

Casas, Penelope. *Delicioso! The Regional Cooking of Spain.* New York: Alfred A. Knopf, 1996.

Cody, William Frederick. *Story of the Wild West and Camp Fire Chats,* Philadelphia and St. Lois: Historical Publishing Company, 1888.

Cone, John Frederick. *Adelina Patti: Queen of Hearts.* Portland, OR: Amadeus Press, 1993.

Dacus, Dr. Joseph A. *The Life and Adventures of Frank and Jesse James.* St. Louis, MO: W.S. Bryan, 1880.

Donaldson, William. Brewer's, *Rogues, Villains and Eccentrics: An A–Z of Roguish Britons through the Ages.* United Kingdom: Wellington House, 2002.

Fleischer, Nat. *The Ring Boxing Encyclopedia and Record Book.* Norwalk, CT: O'Brien Suburban Press, Inc., 1943.

Floyd, Ted, Paul Hess, and George Scott. *Smithsonian Field Guide to the Birds of North America.* New York: HarperCollins, 2008.

Forshaw, Joseph. *Encyclopedia of Birds: A Comprehensive Illustrated Guide by International Experts, Second Edition.* San Diego, CA: Academic Press, 1998.

Gilfoyle, Timothy J. *City of Eros: New York City, Prostitution and the Commercialization of Sex, 1790–1920*. New York: W.W. Norton and Company, 1992.

Gillis, Michael J., and Michael F. Magliari. *John Bidwell and California: The Life and Writings of a Pioneer, 1841–1900*. Spokane, WA: The Arthur H. Clark Company, 2003.

Golway, Terry. *For the Cause of Liberty: A Thousand Years of Ireland's Heroes*. New York: Simon and Schuster, 2000.

Gorn, Elliot J. *The Manly Art: Bare-Knuckle Prize Fighting in America*. Ithaca, NY: Cornell University Press, 1986.

Graff, Henry F. *Grover Cleveland*. New York: Henry Holt and Company, 2002.

Hanley, Ray. *A Place Apart: A Pictorial History of Hot Springs Arkansas*. Fayetteville: University of Arkansas Press, 2011.

Hotten, John Camden. *The Vulgar Words, Street Phrases, and Fast Expressions of High and Low Society. Many with Their Etymology, and a Few with Their History Traced*. London, England: John Camden Hotten, 1864.

Isenberg, Michael T. *John L. Sullivan and His America*. Chicago, IL: University of Illinois, 1988.

Judd, Denis. *Empire: The British Imperial Experience from 1765 to the Present*. London, England: HarperCollins Publishers, 1996.

Kelly, Robert J., Ko-Lin Chin, and Rufus Schatzberg. *Handbook of Organized Crime in the United States*. Santa Barbara, CA: Greenwood Publishing Group, 1994.

Laborde, Peggy Scott, and John Magill. *Canal Street: New Orleans Great Wide Way*. Gretna, LA: Pelican Publishing Company, 2006.

Law Book. *The Southern Reporter, Volume 19: Containing all the Decisions of the Supreme Courts of Alabama, Louisiana, Florida, Mississippi Permanent Edition March 4, 1896 – June 17, 1896*. St. Paul, MN: West Publishing Company, 1896.

Law Book. *The Southwestern Reporter, Volume 11*. St. Paul, MN: West Publishing Co., 1889.

Long, Alecia P. *The Great Southern Babylon: Sex, Race, and Respectability in New Orleans, 1865–1920*. Baton Rouge: Louisiana State University Press, 2004.

Longrigg, Roger. *The History of Horse Racing*. New York: Stein and Day/Publishers, 1972.

Ludy, Robert B. M.D. *Historic Hotels of the World*. Philadelphia, PA: David McKay Company, 1927.

McCarthy, Kieran. *Republican Cobh and the East Cork Volunteers since 1913*. Dublin, Ireland: History Press Ltd, 2008.

McPherson, James. *Battle Cry of Freedom*. New York: Ballantine Books, 1988.

Mee, Bob. *Bare Fists: The History of Bare-Knuckle Prize-Fighting*. Woodstock, NY: Overlook Press, 2001.

Mosley, Charles, ed. *Burke's Peerage and Baronetage Volume 1 of 2*. Crans, Switzerland: Burke's Peerage (Genealogical Books), 1999.

Petzal, David E. *The Encyclopedia of Sporting Firearms*. New York: Oxford Press, 1991.

Purves, William Kirkwood, David Sadava, Gordon H. Orians, and H. Craig Heller. *Life, the Science of Biology*. New York: Macmillan, 2004.

Regan, Gary. *The Bartender's Bible*. New York: HarperCollins, 1991.

Riess, Steven A. *The Sport Kings and the Kings of Crime: Horse Racing, Politics, and Organized Crime*. Syracuse, NY: Syracuse University Press, 2011.

Russell, Don. *The Lives and Legends of Buffalo Bill*. Norman: University of Oklahoma Press, 1960.

Sand, Maurice. *The History of the Harlequinade, Volume I*. London, England: Benjamin Blom Inc., 1915.

Sandall, Robert. *The History of the Salvation Army, Volume I 1865–1878*. Edinburgh, Scotland: Thomas Nelson and Sons Ltd., 1947.

Schwartz, David G. *Roll the Bones: The History of Gambling*. Toronto, Canada: Penguin Group Inc., 2006.

Shamos, Mike. *The Complete Book of Billiards: A Fully Illustrated Reference Guide to the World of Billiards, Pool, Snooker, and Other Cue Sports*. New York: Random House, 1993.

Sherman, William T. *Memoirs of General William T. Sherman*. New York: D. Appleton & Company, 1875.

Slatta, Richard W. *The Cowboy Encyclopedia*. Santa Barbara, CA: ABC-CLIO, 1994.

Smith, Thomas. *The Calcutta Review Vol. LXXII*. London, England: Thomas S. Smith, City Press, 1881.

Stratten and Stratten. *Dublin, Cork, and the South of Ireland: A Literary Commercial and Social Review, Past and Present; with a Description of Leading Mercantile Houses and Commercial Enterprises*. London, England: Stratten and Stratten, 1892.

Strickland, Agnes, and Elizabeth Strickland. *The Lives of the Queens of England, from the Norman Conquest*. London, England: Bell & Daldy, 1868.

Sutton, Judith C. *Champagne and Caviar and Other Delicacies: Celebrate with the Finest Luxuries*. New York: Black Dog and Leventhal Publishers, 1998.

Watson, Kathy. *The Crossing: The Glorious Tragedy of the First Man to Swim the English Channel*. New York: Penguin Putnam Inc., 2000.

Online Resources

Abbott, Karen. "Sin in the Second City." *New York Times*, August 12, 2007. www.nytimes.com/2007/08/12/books/chapters/0812-1st-abbo.html?pagewanted=1&_r=0 (accessed June 16, 2009).

"Anaconda Cocktail Recipe." www.1001cocktails.com/recipes/mixed-drinks/100254/cocktail-anaconda.html (accessed September 21, 2009).

Ancestry Library Edition. "Cambridge University Alumni 1261–1900" http://search.ancestrylibrary.com/search/db.aspx?dbid=3997 (accessed May 5, 2009).

Ancestry Library Edition. "New York Passenger Lists, 1820–1957." http://search.ancestrylibrary.com/search/db.aspx?dbid=7488 (accessed May 5, 2009).

Ancestry Library Edition. "Rasmussen Family Tree." http://trees.ancestrylibrary.com/tree/6814801/person/-1219358644?ssrc= (accessed November 18, 2014).

Ancestry Library Edition. "Sampson Twins Family Tree." http://trees.ancestrylibrary.com/tree/3456757/person/6106404446 (accessed May 5, 2009).

Ancestry Library Edition. "1821–1989 United States City Directories." http://search.ancestrylibrary.com/search/db.aspx?dbid=2469 (accessed September 21, 2009).

Ancestry Library Edition. "1861 England Census." http://search.ancestrylibrary.com/search/db.aspx?dbid=8767 (accessed September 21, 2009).

Ancestry Library Edition. "1870 United States Federal Census." http://search.ancestrylibrary.com/search/db.aspx?dbid=7163 (accessed September 21, 2009).

Ancestry Library Edition. "1880 United States Federal Census." http://search.ancestrylibrary.com/search/db.aspx?dbid=6742 (accessed September 21, 2009).

Ancestry Library Edition. "1930 United States Federal Census Record." http://search.ancestrylibrary.com/search/db.aspx?dbid=6224 (accessed September 21, 2009).

"Animalcules Discovered." http://dimdima.com/science/science_common/show_science.asp?q_aid=88&q_title=Animalcules+Discovered (accessed October 22, 2011).

"Arlington Resort Hotel and Spa, The." www.arlingtonhotel.com (accessed September 23, 2009).

"Balmoral Castle." www.balmoralcastle.com/about.htm (accessed September 21, 2009).

"Cambridge Genealogy: Frederick J. Archer." www.rootsweb.ancestry.com/~engcam/FrederickArcher.htm (accessed September 17, 2011).

"Capitol Hotel, The." www.hotelonline.com/News/PressReleases1998_4th/Oct98_Rice Hotel.html#Rice (accessed June 15, 2009).

"CHAPIN & GORE Chicago, IL. 1870–1918." www.pre-pro.com/midacore/view_vendor.php?vid=ORD4869 (accessed September 21, 2009).

Connor, Patrick. "Bowery St. Bibitor: Martin 'Fiddler' Neary" from http://bloguin.com/queensberryrules/2013-articles/bowery-st-bibitor-martin-fiddler-neary.html (accessed April 17, 2014).

Cyber Boxing Zone. "Arthur Chambers." www.cyberboxingzone.com/boxing/chambers-arthur.htm (accessed April 11, 2009).

Cyber Boxing Zone. "Jack Dempsey." www.cyberboxingzone.com/boxing/non-jack.htm (accessed April 8 2009).

Cyber Boxing Zone. "Joe Fowler." www.cyberboxingzone.com/boxing/JoeFowler.htm (accessed April 8, 2009).

Cyber Boxing Zone. "Billy Leedom." www.cyberboxingzone.com/boxing/leedom-billy.htm (accessed April 8, 2009).

Cyber Boxing Zone. "Charles Lange." www.cyberboxingzone.com/boxing/non-jack.htm (accessed April 8, 2009.)

Cyber Boxing Zone. "George 'Monk' Young." www.cyberboxingzone.com/boxing/JoeFowler (accessed April 8, 2009).

"Daily Event for March 14." www.maritimequest.com/daily_event_archive/2006/march/14_ss_oregon.htm (accessed May 5, 2009).

"Delmonico's Restaurant." www.delmonicosrestaurantgroup.com/restaurant/about-history.html (accessed April 8, 2009).

"Early Days (1878–88), The." www.toffeeweb.com/history/concise/1878-1888.asp (accessed November 23, 2008).

Encyclopedia Britannica. "Cavalla." www.britannica.com/EBchecked/topic/100545/cavalla (accessed September 26, 2011).

Encyclopedia Britannica. "Dotterl." www.britannica.com/EBchecked/topic/169791/dotterel (accessed September 17, 2011).

"Ferdinand A. Abell." www.baseballlibrary.com/ballplayers/player.php?name=Ferdinand_A_Abell (accessed June 6, 2009).

Find a Grave. www.findagrave.com/cgi-bin/fg.cgi?page=gr&GRid=2887 (accessed October 3, 2011).

Florida Memory. "The "Waunita" and an unidentified steamer at Palatka." www.florida memory.com/items/show/149057 (accessed September 15, 2014).

"Former Dealer Hopes for Return of Faro." www.reviewjournal.com/lvrj_home/2000 (accessed October 12, 2008).

"Fort Capron." www.stluciehistoricalsociety.org/capron.html (accessed October 19, 2008).

Free Dictionary, The. "biscuit." www.thefreedictionary.com/biscuit; (accessed September 27, 2011).

"Grand Opera House." http://chicagology.com/rebuilding/rebuilding019/ (accessed September 18, 2014).

Havard Kennedy School. www.hks.harvard.edu/about/history (accessed September 13, 2014).

Hickman, Kennedy. "Franco-Prussian War: Battle of Sedan." http://militaryhistory .about.com/od/battleswars1800s/p/Franco-Prussian-War-Battle-Of-Sedan.htm (accessed October 17, 2011).

History.Net. "Lawmen's Heated Gun Battle in Hot Springs." www.historynet.com/lawmens-heated-gun-battle-in-hot-springs.htm (accessed September 19, 2014).

"History of Holy Trinity Parish." www.neworleanschurches.com/holytrinity/holytrin. htm (accessed September 29, 2009).

"Homesteading Photos from Wyoming Tales and Trails." www.wyomingtalesandtrails .com/agriculture.html (accessed March 8, 2013).

IGFA. www.igfa.org/records/Fish-Records.aspx?Fish=Grouper,%20goliath&LC=ATR (accessed September 22, 2011).

Jensen Beach. www.jensen-beach-florida.com/Jensen-Beach-History.php (accessed April 30, 2009).

Joannides, Paul. "Oral Sex in Another Time." *Boulder Weekly,* http://archive.boulder weekly.com/121505/gettingiton.html (accessed October 20, 2011).

"Louisville and Nashville Railroad." http://railga.com/ln.html (accessed October 17, 2011).

National Police Gazette. http://policegazette.us (accessed September 21, 2009).

New Orleans Public Library. http://nutrias.org/monthly/mar99/mar992.htm (accessed April 28, 2013).

New York Times. "A Blackmailer, Says Divver. He Says Harris, the Lexow Witness, Wrote Threatening Letters," December 5, 1894. http://query.nytimes.com/mem/archive-free/pdf?res=9F04E3DD1231E033A25756C0A9649D94659ED7CF (accessed June 22, 2009).

New York Times. "Another Raid on Chicago Gamblers," June 23, 1884. http://query .nytimes.com/mem/archive-free/pdf?res=980CE4DC123DE533A25750C2A9609 C94659FD7CF (accessed June 6, 2009).

New York Times. "Article 3—No Title," August 16, 1901. http://query.nytimes.com/ mem/archive-free/pdf?res=FB0F12F83F5B11738DDDAF0994D0405B818C F1D3 (accessed April 17, 2013).

New York Times. "Eden Musee Anniversary," April 2, 1885. http://query.nytimes.com/ mem/archive-free/pdf?res=9F02E6DA123DE533A25751C0A9629C94649FD 7CF (accessed June 6, 2009).

New York Times. "How the Wild West Show Has Developed; The First Performance Was on the Fourth of July, 1881. Col. Cody's Success in Europe – How Our Cowboys Proved Their Prowess – Major Burke's Reminiscences," April 7, 1901. http:// query.nytimes.com/mem/archive-free/pdf?res=9B02E3D91E38E733A25754C0A 9629C946097D6CF, (accessed June 6, 2009).

New York Times. "O'Neill's Birthplace Is Marked by Plaque at Times Square Site; O'Neill's Birthplace and Letter He Wrote about It," October 17, 1957. http://query. nytimes.com/gst/abstract.html?res=9F03E1D61038E73ABC4F52DFB667838C6 49EDE (accessed September 16, 2014).

New York Times. "Opening the West Shore," June 5, 1883. http://query.nytimes.com/ mem/archive-free/pdf?res=9401E3D81431E433A25756C0A9609C94629FD7CF &module=Search&mabReward=relbias%3Ar%2C%7B%222%22%3A%22RI%3A1 2%22%7D (accessed June 6, 2009).

New York Times. "The Chicago Gamblers; The Higher Courts to Help in the War against Them," April 3, 1887. http://query.nytimes.com/mem/archive-free/pdf?res= 9506E7D91630E633A25753C1A9629C94669FD7CF (accessed June 6, 2009).

New York Times. "The Hoffman House Sold For $3,500,000; Sixteen-Story Office and Loft Building Will Replace It and the Albemarle. Famous for Half Century Political Headquarters of Democrats in Old Days—Doors to Close Finally on March 15," February 24, 1915. http://query.nytimes.com/mem/archive-free/pdf?res=9D00 E0DE123FE233A25757C2A9649C946496D6CF (accessed June 6, 2009).

"Office of Metro History." www.metrohistory.com/dbpages/NBresults.lasso (accessed April 17, 2013).

Osborne, Ray. "Travel into Time at the Indian River Hotel: Geocache Marks the Spot." www.examiner.com/article/travel-into-time-at-the-indian-river-hotel-geocache-marks-the-spot (accessed April 17, 2013).

"Salvelinus fontinalis (Mitchill, 1814) Brook Trout." www.fishbase.org/summary/Species-Summary.php?id=246 (accessed April 20, 2009).

Ship List, The. www.theshipslist.com/ships/lines/wip.shtml (accessed June 1, 2013).

Smithsonian Marine station at Fort Pierce. "Species Name: Archosargus probatocephalus Common Name:(Sheepshead)." www.sms.si.edu/IRLSpec/Archos_probat.htm (accessed September 22, 2011).

Smithsonian Marine station at Fort Pierce. "Species Name: Lutjanus griseus Common Name: (Mangrove Snapper)." www.sms.si.edu/IRLSpec/Lutjan_griseu.htm (accessed September 22, 2011).

"Southern Hotel, The." www.bbonline.com/mo/southernhotel (accessed September 21, 2009).

"St. James Building." www.jaxhistory.com/Jax%20Arch%20Herit/D-44.htm (accessed October 17, 2011).

"St. Pancras." www.genuki.org.uk/big/eng/MDX/StPancras/StPancrasHistory.html (accessed January 19, 2012).

"William F. Cody Archive, The: Documenting the Life and Times of an American Icon." http://codyarchive.org/memorabilia/wfc.prog.1884.html (accessed February 11, 2014).

WikiAnswers. "How Do You Play Skins Card Game." http://wiki.answers.com/Q/How_do_you_play_Skins_Card_Game (accessed September 26, 2011).

Newspapers and Magazines

Candor. "What of the Faro Banks?" *New York Times,* October 21, 1881, page 3.

City Club of New York. Mayor Low's Administration in New York: The Department of Bridges of the City of New York a Statement of Facts. New York: City Club of New York, 1903.

Daily Inter Ocean. "An Artful Dodger," March 11, 1888, page 1.

Hale, Walter. "The Passing of Old New Orleans," *Uncle Remus's Magazine,* Volume I, March 1908, page 9.

New York Times. "A Raid on the Gamblers; Mr. Whitney Fails to Catch Them His Efforts and Those of Superintendant Walling Frustrated—Timely Warning Given to the Gamblers—How the Work of Fifty Policemen Went for Nothing," January 20, 1880, page 20.

New York Times. "Enter the Crooked Gambler," July 19, 1925, page 17.

New York Times. "Faro Players in Court," April 22, 1877, page 7.

New York Times. "Trying to Recover $54,000 Stolen Money Lost in Gambling Dens," February 26, 1890, page 6.

New Orleans Evening Chronicle. "The Wild West," December 23, 1884, page 1

New Orleans Times-Democrat. "Millionare Cowboys," March 31, 1885, page 4.

Salt Lake Tribune. "Famous Finger Billiardist Turns Up in New York," February 10, 1923, page 12.

San Francisco Call. "Citizens of Portland Credit Mastodon Story," September 12, 1903, page 10.

The Outing: An Illustrated Monthly Magazine of Recreation, Volume 6. "Our Monthly Record," Boston, MA: The Wheelman Company, April to September 1885, page 378.

About the Editor

Kellen Cutsforth is a professional author and has published numerous articles featured in *Wild West* magazine and *Western Writers of America's Roundup* magazine. Kellen is also a member and social media manager for Western Writers of America and the western history group the Denver Posse of Westerners. Along with membership in Western Writers of America, Kellen is also an active member of Westerners International Inc., and the Denver Posse of Westerners. As a member of the Denver Posse of Westerns, he serves as the president of the seventy-year-old organization.

Kellen is a contributor to the Western History blog for the Denver Public Library. His blogs have been featured in "Archives Open" national online periodical. For the past twelve years, Kellen has worked in the manuscript archive of the Western History and Genealogy Department at the Denver Public Library.

ENDNOTES

Introduction

1. Available from http://search.ancestrylibrary.com/cgi-bin/sse.dll?rank=1&new=1&MSAV=1&msT=1&gss=angs-g&gsfn=Evelyn+Thomas+Barton&gsln=Booth&msypn__ftp=Cambridge%2c+Cambridgeshire%2c+England&msypn=82304&msypn_PInfo=8-|0|0|3257|3251|0|0|0|5256|82304|0|&catBucket=rstp&uidh=x14&=y%2c0&_83004003-n_xcl=f&pcat=ROOT_CATEGORY&h=100210&recoff=6+7+8+9&db=alumni6&indiv=1, "Cambridge University Alumni 1261–1900," accessed May 5, 2009.

2. Available from http://search.ancestrylibrary.com/cgi-bin/sse.dll?rank=1&new=1&MSAV=1&msT=1&gss=angs-g&gsfn=Evelyn+&gsln=Booth&msbdy=1860&msddy=1901&msady=1884&msapn__ftp=Sandy+Hook%2c+Monmouth%2c+New+Jersey%2c+USA&msapn=8679&msapn_PInfo=8-%7c0%7c1652393%7c0%7c2%7c3244%7c33%7c0%7c2048%7c8679%7c0%7c&catBucket=rstp&uidh=x14&_83004003-n_xcl=f&pcat=ROOT_CATEGORY&h=10065116&recoff=8+9&db=nypl&indiv=1&ml_rpos=1; "New York Passenger Lists, 1820–1957," accessed May 5, 2009.

3. William Frederick Cody, *Story of the Wild West and Camp Fire Chats* (Philadelphia and St. Louis: Historical Publishing Company, 1888), 699.

4. "Our Monthly Record," *The Outing, Volume 6* (Boston, MA: The Wheelman Company, 1885), 378.

5. Available from http://search.ancestrylibrary.com/iexec?htx=View&r=5542&dbid=7488&iid=NYM237_481-0848&fn=Evelyn&ln=Booth&st=r&ssrc=&pid=10065116; accessed November 18, 2014.

6. William F. "Buffalo Bill" Cody collection, MS 6, Harold McCracken Research Library, Buffalo Bill Historical Center.

7. Sarah J. Blackstone, *The Business of Being Buffalo Bill: Selected Letters of William F. Cody 1879–1917* (New York, NY: Praeger Publishers, 1988), 103.

8. Daily Inter Ocean, page 1, March 11, 1888. "An Artful Dodger."

9. Available from http://search.ancestrylibrary.com/cgi-bin/sse.dll?rank=1&new=1&MSAV=1&msT=1&gss=angs-g&gsfn=Evelyn+&gsln=Booth&msbdy=1860&msddy=1901&msady=1884&msapn__ftp=Sandy+Hook%2c+Monmouth%2c+New+Jersey%2c+USA&msapn=8679&msapn_PInfo=8-%7c0%7c1652393%7c0%7c2%7c3244%7c33%7c0%7c2048%7c8679%7c0%7c&catBucket=rstp&uidh=x14&_83004003-n_xcl=f&pcat=ROOT_CATEGORY&h=24848&recoff=10+11&db=WAdeaths&indiv=1&ml_rpos=24; "Washington Deaths, 1883–1960," accessed May 5, 2009.

10. Available from http://search.ancestrylibrary.com/cgi-bin/sse.dll?rank=1&new=1&MSAV=1&msT=1&gss=angs-g&gsfn=Reginald+Beaumont+&gsln=Heygate&msrpn__ftp=Cambridge%2c+Cambridgeshire%2c+England&msrpn=82304&ms

rpn_PInfo=8-|0|0|3257|3251|0|0|0|5256|82304|0|&catBucket=rstp&uidh=x14&=r
%2c0&_83004003-n_xcl=f&pcat=ROOT_CATEGORY&h=123142&recoff=6+7+8
&db=alumni6&indiv=1; "Cambridge University Alumni 1261–1900," accessed May 5,
2009.
11. Available from http://trees.ancestrylibrary.com/tree/6814801/person/
-1219358644?ssrc=; "Rasmussen Family Tree," accessed November 18, 2014.
12. San Francisco Call, page 10, September 12, 1903. "Citizens of Portland Credit Mastodon Story."
13. Roger Longrigg, *The History of Horse Racing* (New York, NY: Stein and Day/Publish-
ers, 1972), pp. 147–150.
14. Available from http://search.ancestrylibrary.com/cgi-bin/sse.dll?rank=1&new=1&M
SAV=1&msT=1&gss=angs-g&gsfn=Evelyn+&gsln=Booth&msbdy=1860&msddy=1901
&msady=1884&msapn__ftp=Sandy+Hook%2c+Monmouth%2c+New+Jersey
%2c+USA&msapn=8679&msapn_PInfo=8-%7c0%7c1652393%7c0%7c2%7c3244
%7c33%7c0%7c2048%7c8679%7c0%7c&catBucket=rstp&uidh=x14&_83004003-
n_xcl=f&pcat=ROOT_CATEGORY&h=10065116&recoff=8+9&db=nypl&indiv=1
&ml_rpos=1 "New York Passenger Lists, 1820-1957," accessed May 5, 2009.
15. Longrigg, *The History of Horse Racing,* pp. 147–150.

Chapter One: The Journey to America

1. St. Pancras was originally a medieval parish that ran from close to what is now Oxford
Street north as far as Highgate, and from what is now Regent's Park in the west to the
road now known as York Way in the east, boundaries that take in much of the current
London Borough of Camden, including the central part of it. However, St. Pancras has
lost its status as the central settlement in the area. The district now encompassed by the
term St. Pancras is not easy to define, and usage of St. Pancras as a place name is fairly
limited. Available from www.genuki.org.uk/big/eng/MDX/StPancras/StPancras
History.html; accessed January 19, 2012.
2. Liverpool is a city and metropolitan borough of Merseyside, England.
3. The "R.M.S. Oregon" was a Cunard Line steamship that began operation in June,
1884. The vessel would later sink in 1886 after being rammed by a schooner named
"Charles H. Morse." Michael T. Isenberg, *John L. Sullivan and His America* (Chicago:
University of Illinois Press), p. 176, and Michael W. Pocock, "Daily Event for March
14," available from www.maritimequest.com/daily_event_archive/2006/march/14_ss_
oregon.htm; accessed May 5, 2009.
4. The term Norish is in reference to people of Norse, Norwegian, or Scandinavian
ethnicity.
5. "Ditto the purser" refers to the purser or individual who takes care of the ships
accounts and tends to the passengers.
6. Regy is in reference to Reginald Beaumont Heygate (1857–1903).
7. "Frizzle" is in reference to John Percival Frizzle.
8. Brown and Bingham Jack are believed to be references to Reginald Heygate and John
Frizzle.
9. The terms "blind" and "paralytic" are Irish slang for being very drunk.

10. "Gougers" is Irish slang for aggressive males.

11. Madame Adelina Patti (1843–1919) was the highest paid living opera entertainer during her lifetime. She was considered a vocal phenomenon, glamorous figure with both an intriguing professional and private life. At the time of her death, she had been a performer for sixty-three years having made her first appearance in concert at eight years old. At this point in time, she was married to the Marquis of Caux and would be approximately forty-one years old. John Fredrick Cone, Adelina Patti: Queen of Hearts (Portland, OR: Hal Leonard Corporation, 2003) pp. 7, 120.

12. Alfred Greenfield (1853–), a professional boxer and protégé of Richard Kyle Fox, who also gave him thirty British pounds and booked him on the R.M.S Oregon, was an ill-prepared and unskilled prizefighter who was set to fight John L. Sullivan for the Police Gazette Diamond Belt. The belt was riddled in silver and gold with a ring in the center encircled in diamonds. After sustaining a severe beating by Sullivan, the contest was abruptly stopped by New York City Police on December 6, 1884, for "blows with the intent to injure or exhaust either party," which had been ruled an unlawful act by Judge Barrett of the New York State Supreme Court. Isenberg, *John L. Sullivan and His America*, pp. 176–79.

13. The Salvation Army, started as a Christian charity organization by William and Catherine Booth, and had sprung up in East London, England by 1865. William Booth was a minister who preached at Binfeld Road, Clapham, where he would meet Catherine Mumford. The two would later marry and form the Salvation Army. Robert Sandall, The History of the Salvation Army: Volume I 1805–1878 (Edinburgh, Scotland: Thomas Nelson and Sons Ltd., 1947) pp. 1–28.

14. The Liverpool Senior Cup is a soccer competition between the city of Liverpool and the surrounding areas. It is the County Cup Competition of the Liverpool County Football Association. It involves Merseyside, Everton, and Tranmere Rovers. The competition was founded in 1882. "The Early Days (1878–88)," available from www.toffee web.com/history/concise/1878-1888.asp; accessed November 23, 2008.

15. Queenstown, Ireland is known today as Cobh but from 1849–1922 the town was called Queenstown to commemorate a visit by Queen Victoria. Kieran McCarthy, *Republican Cobh and the East Cork Volunteers Since 1913* (Dublin, Ireland: The History Press Ltd, 2008) pp. 62–63.

16. The Queens Hotel was a very prominent hotel in south Ireland. It was built in 1850 and the proprietor at the time was a Mr. W. Raymond. The bedrooms of the hotel accommodated eighty guests and ten distinct sets of sitting rooms. Stratten and Stratten, *Dublin, Cork, and the South of Ireland: A Literary Commercial and Social Review, Past and Present; with a Description of Leading Mercantile Houses and Commercial Enterprises* (London, England: Stratten & Stratten, 1892) p. 233.

17. Bogwood is any wood of trees that have been buried in peat bogs and preserved from decay. Blackthorn Sticks were 2 to 4 foot long Irish shillelaghs made from the Blackthorn Bush that is found throughout Ireland.

18. "Beril" is an Irish slang term used to describe alcoholic beverages.

19. "Batch" is an Irish slang reference to food or to thickly sliced bread.

20. Salvation Dangle Berry's is in reference to the Salvation Army workers on board.

21. "Old Father" is most likely a reference to Mr. James Campbell (1832–); he was a "Scotch merchant"; he was married to Mrs. Campbell and the couple had three children Abigail, Abigail, Alisa. Available from http://search.ancestrylibrary.com/iexec?htx=View &r=5542&dbid=7488&iid=NYM237_481-0848&fn=Evelyn&ln=Booth&st=r&ssrc=& pid=10065116; accessed September 21, 2009.

22. Bruff is a town in east Limerick County, Ireland.

23. Mr. Albert Kaskel (1850–) is located on the first class saloon passenger list as a 34-year-old "German Merchant." "New York Passenger Lists, 1820–1957," available from http://search.ancestrylibrary.com/iexec?htx=View&r=5542&dbid=7488&iid= NYM237_481-0850&fn=Albert&ln=Kaskel&st=r&ssrc=&pid=10065615; accessed September 21, 2009.

24. The term *sooner* is a reference to one of the men's hunting dogs and his "card" is his defecation.

25. Jamaican Ginger was a patent medicine that contained 70 to 80 percent ethyl alcohol by weight. It was nicknamed "Jake" in the United States. Eric Burns, *The Spirits of America: A Social History of Alcohol* (Philadelphia, PA: Temple University Press, 2003) pp. 221–23.

26. H2S refers to hydrogenated sulfur, which is the term the author and his companions use for "passing gas."

27. Miss Minnie Clinton (1862–) is listed as a twenty-two-year-old "spinster" located on the first class saloon passenger list. She appears throughout the journal on numerous occasions and is referred to as Miss Clinton, Minnie, or New York Minnie. "New York Passenger Lists, 1820–1957," available from http://search.ancestrylibrary.com/iexec?htx= View&r=5542&dbid=7488&iid=NYM237_481-0848&fn=Evelyn&ln=Booth&st=r&ssr c=&pid=10065116; accessed September 21, 2009.

28. This is a reference to Mr. Edward O'Connor (1835–) a fifty-year-old Irish merchant. He is also located on the first-class Saloon passenger list. "New York Passenger Lists, 1820–1957," available from http://search.ancestrylibrary.com/iexec?htx=View& r=5542&dbid=7488&iid=NYM237_481-0848&fn=Evelyn&ln=Booth&st=r&ssrc=& pid=10065116; accessed September 21, 2009.

29. The "Anaconda drink" was a combination of whipped cream, brown crème de cacao, crème de menthe, Irish cream, coco rum, and cayenne pepper. "Anaconda Cocktail Recipe," available from www.1001cocktails.com/recipes/mixed-drinks/100254/cocktail -anaconda.html; accessed September 21, 2009.

30. The term "full" is Irish slang for being intoxicated.

31. J. H. Richardson (1849–) is located on the first class saloon passenger list and is listed as a thirty-five-year-old "Rancher." "New York Passenger Lists, 1820–1957." Available from http://search.ancestry.library.com/cgi-bin/sse.dll; accessed September 21, 2009.

32. Mrs. Lillie P W Phipps (1855–) is listed as a twenty-nine-year-old "American wife" on the R.M.S *Oregon's* passenger register. She was born in Kentucky and eventually moved to Queens, New York. She had two children, William and Lillian Phipps. "1930 United States Federal Census Record." Available from http://search.ancestrylibrary.com/ iexec?htx=View&r=5542&dbid=6224&iid=NYT626_1582-0994&fn=Lillie&ln=Phipps &st=r&ssrc=&pid=44916514; accessed September 21, 2009.

Chapter Two: The Falls, Fights, and Big City Nights
1. The Hoffman House Hotel was built and owned by Chicago tobacconist and industry pioneer Edward Hoffman in 1861. The Hoffman House name was also a brand of cigar and a bar. The hotel was frequented by such prominent guests as President Grover Cleveland, U.S. Senator and President of the New York railroad system Chauncey Depew, and famed scout and showman William Frederick "Buffalo Bill" Cody. It ceased operation in 1915. "The Hoffman House Sold for $3,500,000; Sixteen-Story Office and Loft Building Will Replace It and the Albemarle. Famous for half century Political Headquarters of Democrats in Old Days – Doors to Close Finally on March 15." *New York Times,* February 24, 1915. Accessed June 6, 2009. http://query.nytimes.com/mem/archive-free/pdf?res=9D00E0DE123FE233A25757C2A9649C946496D6CF.
2. Mr. John Daily (also spelled Daly) was the proprietor at no. 39 West 28th street. The building was one of the most noted gambling establishments in New York City. It was a five-story brownstone front. Daily was raided several times for gambling improprieties but for the most part the establishment was well respected and heavily frequented by a number of wealthy patrons. "A Raid on the Gamblers; Mr. Whitney Fails to Catch Them His Efforts and those of Superintendant Walling Frustrated–Timely Warning given to the Gamblers–How the Work of Fifty Policemen went for Nothing." *New York Times,* page 8, January 20, 1880. "Enter the Crooked Gambler." *New York Times,* page 17, July 19, 1925. "Trying to Recover $54,000 Stolen Money Lost in Gambling Dens," *New York Times,* page 6, February 26, 1890.
3. Portions of West 29th and 39th streets off of 6th Avenue and Broadway housed a minimum of twelve brothels. And when business was good, it housed at least twenty on such a block. West 39th Street, in particular, had many French-run bordellos and was dubbed the Soubrette Row by the 1890s. These houses became well known all over the country. Timothy Gilfoyle, *City of Eros: New City and the Commercialization of Sex, 1790–1920* (New York, NY: W.W. Norton and Company, 1992), pp. 205, 208.
4. There is no explanation for what Single O or Double O refers to.
5. No information as to who Mr. Read was could be found on the historical record.
6. 5 W 24 was a notorious Faro "rug joint" opened by Henry Price McGrath, a cardsharp from Lexington, Kentucky, who made his name in New Orleans; John Chamberlin, a riverboat gambler from St. Louis, and former heavyweight boxing champion John Morrissey. Steven A. Riess, *The Sport Kings and the Kings of Crime: Horse Racing, Politics, and Organized Crime* (Syracuse, NY: Syracuse University Press, 2011) pp. 22–23.
7. Ferdinand A. Abell was proprietor at No. 818 Broadway in New York. He was one of the original founders of the Brooklyn Dodgers and put up most of the money for the team in 1883. He also financed the building of Washington Park the original home of the Dodgers. He won two pennants and then consolidated with Baltimore in 1889. He was primarily a Rhode Island casino owner for the majority of his career. "Fedinand A. Abell," available from www.baseballlibrary.com/ballplayers/player.php?name=Ferdinand_A_Abell; accessed June 6, 2009.
8. After 1850, Broadway had become the axis of entertainment and the sex district in the city. Eight blocks along Broadway was awash with designer clothing stores such as Brooks Brothers, Lord and Taylor, Tiffany, and Matthew Brady as well as many houses

of prostitution. Gilfoyle, *City of Eros: New City and the Commercialization of Sex, 1790–1920*, p. 120.

9. Kirk Gunn, who along with Cy James and Jim Crawford were the proprietors of the gambling house at 98 Randolph Street in Chicago, Illinois. In June of 1884 a directive by Mayor Harrison led to many clients of the establishment being arrested. "Another Raid on Chicago Gamblers." *New York Times,* June 23, 1884. Accessed June 6, 2009. http://query.nytimes.com/mem/archive-free/pdf?res=980CE4DC123DE533A25750C2 A9609C94659FD7CF.

10. Gambling houses in Chicago were so extensive in the block between Randolph, Clark, and State streets that the area was known as "Hair Trigger Block" because so many shootings happened over disagreements stemming from problems in the gambling houses and brothels. Robert J. Kelly, Ko-Lin Chin, and Rufus Schatzberg, *Handbook of Organized Crime in the United States* (Santa Barbara, CA: Greenwood Publishing Group, 1994), p. 172.

11. Jefferson Hankins, who along with John Dowling and Samuel Dall ran a well-known gambling establishment at 125 Clark Street in Chicago, Illinois. In 1887 the three would swindle Bobby Caruthers, well-known pitcher for the St. Louis Browns, out of $9,000 and would be searched and have their establishment turned upside down by local law enforcement. "The Chicago Gamblers. The Higher Courts to Help in the War against Them." *New York Times,* April 9, 1887. Accessed June 6, 2009. http://query.nytimes .com/mem/archive-free/pdf?res=9506E7D91630E633A25753C1A9629C94669FD7CF.

12. No information as to who Hynes was could be found on the historical record.

13. 119 Clark Street in Chicago, Illinois, is a reference to the Chicago Grand Opera House. The building stood on 119 North Clark Street from 1872–1958. It was built upon the original site of Bryan Hall and Hooley's Opera House. J. A. Hamlin and brother (L. B. Hamlin) purchased the property in January 1872 and erected the first building that was completed upon that block after a fire destroyed the original building. In 1873, the Hamlin Brothers built upon the rear lot what was subsequently known as Foley's Billiard Hall, which was at the time the largest billiard hall in the world, containing thirty tables on one floor. In 1874, the billiard hall property passed out of the hands of Mr. Foley into the hands of Hamlin Bros., and the billiard business was discontinued after a few months and the hall reconstructed, with an additional building added to the east end. "Grand Opera House," available from http://chicagology.com/rebuilding/rebuilding019/; accessed September 18, 2014.

14. Charles F. Bush (1836–) was a saloon owner with his family in New Orleans. He was married to Jennie F. Bush and they had one child, Anny Bush. "1870 United States Federal Census," available from http://search.ancestry.library.com/cgi-bin/sse.dll; accessed September 21, 2009.

15. St. Charles Avenue/Street was at one time one of New Orleans most prominent and finest thoroughfares. It was not immune to prostitution, however, as several concert saloons appeared on the street. Alecia P. Long, *The Great Southern Babylon: Sex, Race, and Respectability in New Orleans 1865–1920.* (Baton Rouge: Louisiana State University Press, 2004), p. 82.

16. Concert saloons and brothels began springing up on Royal Street in the early 1870s and

in the decade to follow would dominate several city blocks in New Orleans. Royal Street held the St. Louis Hotel, which was described as a "kind of homosocial pleasure dome with overlapping commercial and leisure attractions." Women were always in the area as both commodities and as privileged free women both black and white. Long, *The Great Southern Babylon: Sex, Race, and Respectability in New Orleans 1865–1920*, pp. 63, 83–85.

17. Bud Renaud was a New Orleans boxing promoter, gambler, and business partner of Patrick Duffy who was the promoter for heavy weight champion John L. Sullivan. He, along with Duffy, bucked an anti-boxing sentiment that was rampant at the time in New Orleans to amass a small fortune promoting bouts that fans and attendees paid in advance for not knowing where the fight would take place or when it would happen. Isenberg, *John L. Sullivan and His America*, pp. 266–69.

18. Mrs. Emily Burgess was the wife of John T. Burgess, commercial editor, *American Grocer and Dry Goods Chronicle*. She is referred to by Doc as Miss B, Burgy or Buriggins. "New York Passenger Lists, 1820–1957," available from http://search.ancestry.library.com/cgi-bin/sse.dll; accessed September 21, 2009.

19. The "crack" or "craic," as it is also referred to is Irish slang for someone telling a story or a piece of gossip.

20. The Eden Musee was a waxwork and museum originating in 1883. It was popular in the latter half of the nineteenth century in Europe as well as America. At the time, the museum featured two new additions. One for the U.S. Presidents that included George Washington and Grover Cleveland, and another showing the five top Irish patriots of the day: O'Connell, Butt, Emmet, Davitt, and Parne. "Eden Musee Anniversary." *New York Times*, April 2, 1885. Accessed June 9, 2009. http://query.nytimes.com/mem/archive-free/pdf?res=9F02E6DA123DE533A25751C0A9629C94649FD7CF.

21. The Winter Garden was located at 624 Broadway in New York, New York. It was originally known as the Old Bowery Theatre but closed for renovation in July of 1859. When the theater reopened it boasted a 100-foot stage and other alterations that were said to have cost $20,000. It became known as the Winter Garden Theatre on September 14, 1859. T. Allston Brown, *The History of the New York Stage: From the First Performance in 1732 to 1901, Vol. I* (New York: Dodd, Mead and Company, 1903), p. 446

22. JPF is the signature that traveling companion Dr. John Percival Frizzle uses to identify himself.

23. "Mr. Barrett's" most likely refers to the Barrett House Hotel. The Hotel, built in 1883, stood on the northeast corner of 43rd Street in New York City. It was centered in what was then known as Longacre Square (now known as Times Square). In 1888, the hotel was the site where Nobel Prize–winning playwright Eugene O'Neill was born. *New York Times*, "O'Neill's Birthplace Is Marked by Plaque at Times Square Site; O'Neill's Birthplace and Letter He Wrote about It." *New York Times*, October 17, 1957. Accessed September 16, 2014. http://query.nytimes.com/gst/abstract.html?res=9F03E1D61038E73ABC4F52DFB667838C649EDE.

24. Jimmy Kelly, with former heavyweight boxer Jerry Murphy, in 1883 would form a boxing act where they would put on exhibition fights that would be met with great success. The two men would eventually be hired by Sam Hague to travel with his minstrel band in Great Britain. "The Ring," available from http://idnc.library.illinois.edu/cgi-bin/

illinois?a=d&d=NYC18840823.2.102#; accessed September 15, 2014.

25. Tom Allen (1840–1904) was born in Birmingham, England. He was five feet eleven inches tall and weighed 175 lbs. As a prizefighter he was a championship contender. In 1870, he would lose a championship fight in a one-sided contest in ten rounds to Jem Mace of Norfolk. Allen would win the American Championship in 1869. Bob Mee, *Bare Fists: The History of Bare Knuckle Prize Fighting* (New York: The Overlook Press, 2001), pp. 172, 177.

26. John L. Sullivan (1847–1918), known as the "Boston Strong Boy" or the "Highland Boy," was an American heavyweight boxer and the Heavyweight Champion of the World. Sullivan became champion in 1882 by defeating then champion Paddy Ryan, who incidentally would become his lifelong nemesis. Sullivan was well muscled, powerful, and aggressively violent. He would later retire with a record of 35-1-2. His lone defeat relinquished his heavyweight title to "Gentleman" James Corbett in 1892 via knockout. Mee, *Bare Fists: The History of Bare Knuckle Prize Fighting*, pp. 180–98.

27. The "Professor" John Laflin also nicknamed the "Society Adonis," was a fighter with many wealthy friends in New York society. This brought a great fan following to his fights. He was slightly larger than Sullivan but was totally out of shape and Sullivan was obviously the better fighter. It is reported that the three-round bout was well received and ended with Laflin receiving quite a beating. Isenberg, *John L. Sullivan and His America*, p. 127.

28. Paddy Ryan (1853–1900) born in Thurles, he was the youngest of eleven children. As a former prize fighter and bare-knuckle champion, he was known as the "Trojan Giant." He lost his heavyweight title to John L. Sullivan in 1882 via knockout in the ninth round. A nemesis of Sullivan's, the two would rematch in 1885 only to have the fight stopped by police for "slugging" and not "sparing." Elliot J. Gorn, *The Manly Art: Bare Knuckle Prize Fighting in America* (Ithica, NY: Cornell University Press, 1986) pp. 211–15.

29. Katharine and Jaffray could not be found on the historical record.

30. Kummel is a liqueur flavored with distilled caraway seeds. Gary Regan, The Bartender's Bible (New York: Harper Collins Publishers Inc., 1991), p. 270.

31. Jerry Murphy was a local New York boxer who, in 1880, would have an exhibition with John L. Sullivan. His fame never reached a greater height. Mee, *Bare Fists: The History of Bare Knuckle Prize Fighting,* p. 181.

32. The Sharps Long rifle was a single-shot breech-loader that utilized paper cartridges. It ceased production in 1881. David E. Petzal, *The Encyclopedia of Sporting Firearms* (New York: Oxford University Press, 1991), p. 292.

33. The Brunswick Hotel was located at 225 Fifth Avenue on Madison Square Park. It was heavily favored by English tourists. It was torn down around 1904. Available from, www.metrohistory.com/dbpages/NBresults.lasso; accessed April 17, 2013.

34. No information as to who Mrs. Hammond could be found on the historical record.

35. Martin "Fiddler" Neary (1848–1903) was a former prize fighter and convicted felon. He was sentenced to prison for manslaughter and would later die at the age of forty-five from pneumonia at New York's Bellevue Hospital. He was buried at Calvary Cemetery. Before that, he worked as a policeman on Coney Island. Patrick Connor,

"Bowery St. Bibitor: Martin 'Fiddler' Neary," available from http://bloguin.com/queensberryrules/2013-articles/bowery-st-bibitor-martin-fiddler-neary.html; accessed April 17, 2013.

36. Jack Keenan was a former prize fighter who would be knocked out in two rounds by Jack "Nonpareil" Dempsey in 1885 in San Francisco, California. Nat Fleischer, *The Ring Boxing Encyclopedia and Record Book* (Norwalk, CT: O'Brien Suburban Press, Inc. 1943), p. 138.

37. Joe Fowler (? –1892) was a 135 lbs. featherweight champion from Bristol, England. He was known for his quickness and skilled boxing technique. He arrived in America in 1880 and would fight in many boxing exhibitions. He would fight George "Monk" Young four times before his career would end. "Joe Fowler," available from www.cyber-boxingzone.com/boxing/JoeFowler.htm; accessed April 8, 2009.

38. George "Monk" Young was an American boxer from Brooklyn, New York. He would fight English Champion Joe Fowler on four separate occasions in (specific months disputed) 1884, 1886, and twice in 1888. Three of the four would be exhibition contests and the fourth would end in a "no decision." "Joe Fowler," available from www.cyberboxing zone.com/boxing/JoeFowler.htm; accessed April 8, 2009.

39. Jack "Nonpareil" Dempsey (1862–1895) was an Irish champion lightweight and middleweight boxer who was one of the most popular fighters of the day. He was born John Edward Kelly. He would lose his middleweight crown in 1890 in New Orleans to Australian challenger Bob Fitzsimmons. He finished his career with a record of 62-3-0. Dempsey would die at the age of thirty-three from tuberculosis. Isenberg, *John L. Sullivan and His America,* pp. 307, 313.

40. Tom Ferguson was a local fighter from New York who on November 10, 1884 (some records report November 6, 1884) lost to Jack "Nonpareil" Dempsey. Fleischer, *The Ring Boxing Encyclopedia and Record Book,* p. 138.

41. Billy Edwards (1844–1907) was a celebrated lightweight champion boxer nicknamed "Make-Believe Billy." Edwards began boxing at the age of fourteen and fought Sam Collyer on August 24, 1868, for the American Lightweight Championship. Edwards won the fight in the 34th-round. Edwards fought Hall of Famer Charlie Mitchell in 1884, losing in the 3rd round. Following the Mitchell bout, Edwards retired from the ring but remained in boxing by training John L. Sullivan for several winning contests. Mee, *Bare Fists: The History of Bare Knuckle Prize Fighting,* p. 177.

42. "Sandy" drink refers to a mixed drink that contains rum, vermouth, brandy, lemon juice, and sugar. Regan, *The Bartender's Bible,* p. 129.

43. Sir George William Beaumont (1851–1914) was 10th Baronet of Stoughton Grange County, in Leicester. He was given his title June 8, 1882. In 1880, he was married to Lillie Ellen, the second daughter of Major-General George Ayton Craster. Charles Mosley, editor, *Burke's Peerage and Baronetage Volume 1 of 2* (Crans, Switzerland: [Genealogical Books] Ltd. 1999), p. 230.

44. Bridget Butler (1855–) was a housekeeper of Irish descent who was married to John Butler and was most likely employed as a maid at the Hoffman House. "1880 United States Federal Census," available from http://search.ancestry.library.com/cgi-bin/ssc.dll; accessed September 21, 2009.

45. Miss Evelyn Bell was a madam and proprietor of 65, 67, 69, and 71 West 36th Street. She, for some years, paid protection to the police of New York that totaled the sum of $100,000. She later testified against the police in 1895. "A Blackmailer, Says Divver.; He Says Harris, the Lexow Witness, Wrote Threatening Letters." *New York Times,* December 5, 1894. Accessed June 22, 2009. http://query.nytimes.com/mem/archive-free/pdf.

46. No reference to who "Lulu" was could be found on the historical record.

47. "Tosser" is British slang for someone that is an idiot.

48. Pommery is a French Champagne that is made in the town of Remis, France. Judith C. Sutton, *Champagne and Caviar and Other Delicacies* (New York: Black Dog and Leventhal Publishers, Inc., 1998), p. 14.

49. Del's refers to Delmonico's Restaurant, opened in 1837 as America's first fine-dining restaurant, and continues to operate today serving the connoisseur of fine American food in its premier location at 56 Beaver Street, the heart of Manhattan's financial district on Fourteenth Street. It is the birthplace of the Delmonico Steak, Delmonico Potatoes, Eggs Benedict, Lobster Newburg, and Baked Alaska. Available from www.delmonicos restaurantgroup.com/about-firsts.html; accessed April 8, 2009.

50. Jack is a reference to John Frizzle.

51. Embileing Brom refers to regurgitating.

52. West Shore Railroad was a railroad that ran from Weehawken, New Jersey, across the Hudson River to New York City, then along the west shore of the river to Albany, New York, and north to Buffalo, New York. "Opening the West Shore." *New York Times,* June 5, 1883. Accessed May 2, 2013. http://query.nytimes.com/mem/archive-free/pdf?res=94 01E3D81431E433A25756C0A9609C94629FD7CF&module=Search&mabReward=re lbias%3Ar%2C%7B%222%22%3A%22RI%3A12%22%7D.

53. This is a reference to the John L. Sullivan vs. Alfred Greenfield contest in which Mayor Franklin Edison prohibited the fight because the events would be "disgraceful to the city." The two fighters were arrested and the match was later rescheduled for December 6, 1884. The rematch was stopped a second time and the two were once again arrested for trying to "knock each other out." Isenberg, *John L. Sullivan and His America,* pp. 176–79.

54. No information for Dr. Wright could be found on the historical record.

55. Eileen is the name of the men's pregnant hunting dog.

56. Jay Gould (1846–1892), an American railroad financier, controlled the Northern Pacific Railroad and helped to instigate a shooting war between the United States and Canada. He was one of the nineteenth century's most notorious share swindlers. William Donaldson, *Brewer's Rogues, Villains and Eccentrics: An A–Z of Roguish Britons through the Ages* (London, England: Wellington House, 2002), p. 291.

57. *Camps in the Rockies* was first self published in 1882 by William Adolph Baillie-Groham.

58. No information as to who Mr. Read was could be found on the historical record.

59. Jerome Park was founded by Leonard W. Jerome and August Belmont. It would host the Belmont Stakes, the oldest of the American triple crown races, from 1866–1890 along with many other racing events. Longrigg, *The History of Horse Racing,* pp.

222–24.

60. It is known that John L. Sullivan's appeal began to meander at this time because of his excessive drinking and marital problems that were made very public. Mee, *Bare Fists: The History of Bare Knuckle Prize Fighting*, pp. 194–95.

61. Vin Brut Champagne is a French Pommery. Sutton, *Champagne and Caviar and Other Delicacies*, p. 14.

62. French to English translation of "Max Greges" is Max Greger which was a Hungarian producer of champagne. Thomas Smith, *The Calcutta Review Vol. LXXII* (London, England: Thomas S. Smith, City Press, 1881), p. iv.

63. Miss Hastings is a reference to Caroline Hastings, who was also known as Kate or Catherine and also identified as Carrie by the author. She had become a prominent prostitute by the mid nineteenth century. At this point in time she would be much older and would most likely be a proprietor of a brothel. She was famous for attacking the editor and writer Ned Buntline for slandering her in his newspaper and also for throwing lavish prostitute-filled masquerade balls. Timothy J. Gilfoyle, *City of Eros: New York City, Prostitution and the Commercialization of Sex, 1790–1920* (New York: W.W. Norton and Company, 1992), pp. 130, 144–45.

64. No information as to who Col. Early was could be found on the historical record.

65. Arthur Chambers (1846–1923) was a boxer who was born in Lancashire England. He fought at 125 pounds and won the Lightweight Championship of America in 1872, a fight in which he defeated Billy Edwards. He would also referee a fight between George Fryer and Billy Leedom in 1885. He was a member of both the Ring Boxing Hall of Fame and the International Boxing Hall of Fame. "Arthur Chambers," Available from www.cyberboxingzone.com/boxing/chambers-arthur.htm; accessed April 11, 2009.

66. "Professor" Mike Donovan (1847–1918) was acknowledged as a ring genius and had a career that spanned from 1866–1891. During that time, he fought both John L. Sullivan and Jack "Nonpariel" Dempsey. He would eventually publish a book called *The Science of Boxing* in 1893. Famed lawman Wyatt Earp was a time keeper for a fight that Donovan was a corner man for. Mee, *Bare Fists: The History of Bare Knuckle Prize Fighting*, pp. 180–82, 192.

67. Jacob is the name of the police detective that Booth encountered earlier.

68. 108 West 31st was a known gambling establishment and brothel. It would be raided several times by the New York City police over the years. *Mayor Low's Administration in New York: The Department of Bridges of the City of New York A Statement of Facts* (New York: City Club of New York, 1903), p. 35.

69. An Agnus Dei is a Sacramental, small disc of round or oval wax impressed with a lamb normally blessed by the Catholic Pope. Robert Broderick, *The Catholic Encyclopedia* (Nashville, TN: Thomas Nelson Inc.), p. 28.

70. Sooner is a reference to a new hunting dog that the men have acquired.

71. Kingston is in Ulster County New York. It is located about 91 miles from New York City.

72. Goat Island is a strip of land that causes the Niagara River to split into two channels separating the American Falls on the western side. The river then makes an abrupt ninety degree turn creating the Horseshoe Falls nearer to the Canadian side. The island

is created of silts and clays that had originally lain on the bottom of the vanished Lake Tonawanda. Pierre Berton, *Niagara: A History of the Falls* (New York: McClelland and Stewart Inc., 1992), p. 9.

73. The Spencer House was located on the American side of Niagara Falls. On May 1, 1887, the hotel would serve as the auction house for the sale of the first "hydraulic canal" and would be bought by Jacob Schoellkopf, a Buffalo tanner and miller, for $67,000. Pierre Berton, *Niagara: A History of the Falls* (New York: McClelland and Steward Inc., 1992), p. 154.

74. G.I.H. is in reference to Goat Island House.

75. Prospect Park was also known as Prospect Point. It was a popular rock vantage point right across from Table Rock on the American side of Niagara Falls. In 1954, the majority fell into the falls from being weathered by erosion. Berton, *Niagara: A History of the Falls*, p. 6.

76. Captain Matthew Webb (1848–1883) was the first man to swim the English Channel in 1875. He would later try and duplicate his swimming feat by trying to ford the Niagara River in Niagara Falls, New York, in 1883, but would drown in his attempt. Kathy Watson, *The Crossing* (New York: Headline Book Publishing, 2000), pp. 229–30.

77. Table Rock was a huge dolostone several acres in size that once hung over the gorge near the lip of the Horseshoe Falls. It was the favorite vantage point for tourists and photographers. Over the last century the rocks beneath it weathered, and it finally plummeted into the falls. Berton, *Niagara: A History of the Falls*, pp. 73, 121.

78. The Burning Spring was a popular destination spot for tourists and was near the Horseshoe Falls. It had large amounts of sulphur water that was taken and sold to tourists. Berton, Niagara: A History of the Falls, pp. 73, 121.

79. Stephen Grover Cleveland (1837–1908) was the twenty-second and twenty-fourth president of the United States. He was elected as a pro-business Democrat and won praise for his honesty, integrity, independence, and his commitment to the principals of classical liberalism. He has the distinction of being the only president elected to two nonconsecutive terms. Henry F. Graff, *Grover Cleveland* (New York: Henry Holt and Company, LLC, 2002) pp. 140–41.

Chapter Three: Hunting Thrills and Buffalo Bill

1. Chatham-Kent, Canada, is approximately thirty miles northeast of Detroit, Michigan.

2. Auburn, Michigan is approximately 322 miles south of Chicago, Illinois.

3. The Palmer House erected by Potter Palmer, a pioneer in the dry goods business, originally burned to the ground in 1871. The hotel was resurrected in 1873 and was constructed of brick and iron to create a more fire retardant structure. The hotel became host to Generals U. S. Grant and Philip Sheridan, President Roscoe Conklin, author Rudyard Kipling, and many other distinguished guests. Robert B. Ludy, M.D. *Historic Hotels of the World* (Philadelphia, PA: David McKay Company, 1927), p. 259.

4. No information as to what "Cook's" was could be found on the historical record.

5. Union General Phillip H. Sheridan (1831–1888), known as the commandant was a small bandy-legged man whose only distinctions before the American Civil War had been pugnacity and a handlebar mustache. He was known for his ferocity in battle

and control of a field cavalry unit and was soon promoted to brigade command. James McPherson, *Battle Cry of Freedom* (New York: Ballantine Books, 1988), p. 519.

6. No information as to who Barnett was could be found on the historical record.

7. This is either in reference to Sioux City, Iowa; Nebraska; or South Dakota.

8. Bonaparte "Boney" Earnest (1845–) was a well-known scout and frontiersman living in Carbon County, Wyoming, at the turn of the century. He served as an army scout along with Tom Sun under Anson Mills in the Powder River campaign of 1876. "Homesteading Photos from Wyoming Tales and Trails," available from www.wyomingtalesandtrails.com/agriculture.html and "United State Federal Census," http://search.ancestrylibrary.com/cgi-bin/sse.dll?db=1930usfedcen&indiv=try&h=113179727; accessed March 8, 2013.

9. Snipe is a wading bird, genus *Rostratula*; they prefer tropical lowlands and swamps and are camouflaged to avoid predators. Joseph Forshaw, Encyclopedia of Birds (San Diego, CA: Academic Press, 1991), pp. 34, 107.

10. This is either a reference to Christiana, Tennessee, or Christiana, Pennsylvania.

11. Poteen pronounced, PO-CHEEN, is a Gaelic word meaning "in a pot" and refers to any unlawfully distilled spirit. Regan, *The Bartender's Bible*, p. 206.

12. Carrie Watson's was a brothel located at 441 Clark Street in Chicago, Illinois. It was located in a vice neighborhood called "Little Cheyenne"; the house was elegant and was known world-wide. Its owner, Madame Watson, was revered by Chicago leaders and left alone by police. Karen Abbott, "Sin in the Second City." *New York Times*, August 12, 2007. Available from www.nytimes.com/2007/08/12/books; accessed June 16, 2009.

13. Chapin and Gore (1870–1918) was a bar and distillery in Chicago. It was also popular in Kentucky, Kansas City, Indianapolis, and France. This particular one was located on Monroe Street in Chicago from 1873–1902. Available from www.pre-pro.com/midacore/view_vendor.php?vid=ORD4869; accessed September 21, 2009.

14. Emma Johnson was a prostitute in the late 1800s. She was notorious for oral sex. The term "French" that was often attributed to several brothels identified oral sex as a specialty of the house. Emma Johnson also had live sex circuses where male performers dressed in long manes and wore tails. Paul Joannides, *Boulder Weekly*, "Oral Sex in Another Time." Available from http://archive.boulderweekly.com/121505/gettingiton.html; accessed October 20, 2011.

15. No information as to who Bell Demmick was could be found on the historical record.

16. "Spanish Stew" is most likely a reference to Gazpacho, native to Andalucia. It is prepared with bread, garlic, salt, olive oil, vinegar, and water. Penelope Casas, *Delicioso! The Regional Cooking of Spain* (New York: Alfred A. Knopf, Inc., 1996), p. 341.

17. Patrick Sheedy had taken over as John L. Sullivan's manager in early 1884. He was known as a brash gambler and loud mouth. He set up the match between Sullivan and Laflin to benefit the autumn flood victims of Ohio in a great show of charity. It is one reason, among many, why the Sullivan v. Laflin contest was so successful. Isenberg, *John L. Sullivan and His America*, p. 174.

18. The Southern Hotel is located in Sainte Genevieve, Missouri, and about fifty-three miles away from St. Louis. It is known as the oldest hotel in America west of the

Mississippi River and has operated as a hotel since 1805. "The Southern Hotel," available from www.southernhotelbb.com/sohotelhistory.htm; accessed September 21, 2009.

19. Weiner, Arkansas, is a small town around 109 miles northeast of Little Rock, Arkansas.

20. The Stevens-Lord single-shot .22 pistol or rifle was manufactured in the early 1850s by J.C. Stevens Company. David E. Petzal, *The Encyclopedia of Sporting Firearms* (New York: Oxford University Press, 1991), p. 318.

21. Pyramids is a single-rack pocket billiard game played with fifteen red balls and a cue ball. The English version is played with what is called "Baulk Semicircle" and fifteen red balls. Mike Shamos, *The Complete Book of Billiards: A Fully Illustrated Reference Guide to the World of Billiards, Pool, Snooker, and Other Cue Sports* (New York: Gramercy Books, 1993), p. 184.

22. *Vie De Mais*—French to English translation in this context means "make no attempt to find-life-in-town."

23. Fisher, Arkansas, is located in Poinsett County and is approximately ten miles south of Weiner, Arkansas.

24. Swan Lake, Arkansas, is approximately 125 miles southeast of Fisher, Arkansas.

25. Balmoral is a Scottish hunting manor. It was built by Sir William Drummond in 1390 and was owned by King Robert II. It was frequently used as a hunting lodge. Available from www.balmoralcastle.com/about.htm; accessed October 20, 2011.

26. This entry and following events may have occurred a little earlier in December or even in late November. Buffalo Bill Cody was in the area and was heading to a performance with his Wild West in Helena, Arkansas, that is south of Weiner, Arkansas. Cody was in Helena around December 1 or 2. There is also a possibility that this individual is not the William Frederick "Buffalo Bill" Cody. Given that Booth and his friends have a propensity for nicknaming, it is possible that they met a companion who they also nicknamed "Buffalo Bill." When Booth and his companions eventually do meet the actual Buffalo Bill Cody in New Orleans they are "formally" introduced to him and do not seem to have been acquainted with him previously.

27. This is possibly Colonel William Fredrick "Buffalo Bill" Cody (1846–1917) who was a frontiersman, scout, buffalo hunter, and entertainer. He became one of the central icons of the American Frontier, And incredibly famous when he created Buffalo Bill's Wild West Show. Richard W. Slatta, *The Cowboy Encyclopedia* (Santa Barbara, CA: ABC-CLIO, 1994), p. 72.

28. Brinkley, Arkansas, is approximately fifty-four miles South of Weiner, Arkansas.

29. Hickory Ridge, Arkansas, is a town approximately sixteen miles south of Weiner, Arkansas.

30. No information for Mrs. Maloney could be found on the historical record.

31. Tilton, Arkansas, is located approximately six miles south of Hickory Ridge, Arkansas.

32. Whist is a card game normally played socially amongst four participants. The game arrived in England around the 1660s. It is normally known as a trick-taking card game; play centers around a series of finite rounds or units of play. David G. Schwartz, *Roll the Bones: The History of Gambling* (New York: Penguin Group, 2006) pp. 162–68.

33. Hunter, Arkansas, is approximately twenty-five miles south of Hickory Ridge,

Arkansas.

34. Gus and Dan are the names of the ponies bought by Reginald Heygate.

35. Hot Springs, Arkansas, is approximately 148 miles south of Tilton, Arkansas.

36. Little Rock, Arkansas, is approximately ninety-seven miles south of Tilton, Arkansas.

37. The Arlington Hotel is located in the Ouachita Mountains of what is now Hot Springs National Park. It first opened in 1875. "The Arlington Resort Hotel and Spa," available from www.arlingtonhotel.com; accessed September 23, 2009.

38. "White Pine" Russell was a gambler and bunko operator who had recently been arrested in April of 1884 for fleecing a Colorado man out of $400. He would later be released for returning $150 of the original stolen amount. Herbert Asbury, *The French Quarter: An Informal History of New Orleans Underworld* (New York: Thunder's Mouth Press, 1936), p. 399.

39. Captain Charles Bowling (1841–) was a close friend of Fred Archer's and was present when Archer died. He and Archer traveled from Liverpool, England, to New York on the steamship *Bothnia* on November 26, 1884. He resided at the Junior United Services Club in London, which was a gentleman's club for army and navy officers over the rank of major and commander. He was forty-three years old when he and Archer came to New York. He is often referred to in the journal as "Cap" or "Captain." Available from www.rootsweb.ancestry.com/~engcam/FrederickArcher.htm; accessed September 17, 2011.

40. Throughout the 1870s and 1880s Hot Springs, Arkansas, known for the natural warm spring waters had also become a hot spot for gambling and prostitution. By the late 1870s, gambling, which probably existed in Hot Springs as early as 1849, had become a local growth industry that rivaled the healing waters. The town was controlled by two gambling factions known as the Flynns and the Dorans. The Flynns were run by Frank "Boss Gambler" Flynn who controlled the majority of brothels and gambling establishments on Hot Springs Central Avenue. His businesses were challenged by Major S. A. Doran, a Confederate veteran who had opened gambling establishments in the same neighborhood. A gunfight between the two sides erupted in February 1884. The two factions owned several saloons and Shipley's most likely belongs to one of them. Available from www.historynet.com/lawmens-heated-gun-battle-in-hot-springs.htm; accessed September 19, 2014.

41. Written by Dr. Joseph Dacus, *The Life and Adventures of Frank and Jesse James: Noted Western Outlaws* (St. Louis, MO: W.S. Bryan, 1880).

42. "Daniel Barret's" refers to the Palace Bath House and gambling establishment. Daniel Barrett was a clerk at the Palace Bath House. It was built in 1880 and owned by Jim Lane, a gambling entrepreneur from Illinois. He was later pushed out by Frank Flynn's mob and the Palace was taken over in 1884 by Major S. A. Doran, who competed directly with Flynn. Ray Hanley, *A Place Apart: A Pictorial History of Hot Springs Arkansas* (Fayetteville: University of Arkansas Press, 2011), p. 30. Available from http://search.ancestrylibrary.com/cgi-bin/sse.dll?rank=1&new=1&MSAV=0&msT=1&gss=angs-c&gsfn=Daniel&gsln=Barrett&mswpn__ftp=Arkansas%2c+USA&mswpn=6&mswpn_PInfo=5-%7c0%7c1652393%7c0%7c2%7c3246%7c6%7c0%7c0%7c0%7c0%7c&uidh=x14&pcat=37&h=792952368&db=USDirectories&indiv=1&ml_rpos=2; accessed

September 19, 2014.

43. Mr. John Farin (1830–) was a former sailor of Irish descent. He lived with his wife Rose Ann Farin and their five children. Available from "1880 United States Census," available from http://search.ancestry.library.com/cgi-bin/sse.dll; accessed September 21, 2009.

44. The tarantula's bile or digestive juices are secreted to dissolve its meal because the tarantula can only eat that which is in liquid form.

45. Sol is the name of a hunting dog.

46. *Salvelinus Fontinalis* is a name for a common brook trout that is found in many North American rivers, creeks and streams. It feeds on a wide range of organisms from crustaceans to worms and insects. Available from www.fishbase.org/summary/Species Summary.php?id=246; accessed April 20, 2009.

Chapter Four: A Very Merry New Year

1. Sulphur, Texas, is approximately nine miles south of Texarkana, Texas.

2. Malvern, Arkansas, is approximately twenty-two miles southeast of Hot Springs, Arkansas.

3. Eton, England, is approximately twenty-three miles west of London, England.

4. *The National Police Gazette* was a magazine founded in 1845 by Enoch Camp and George Wilkes. It was a tabloid paper that covered murders, Wild West outlaws, and sports. It was well known for its engravings of scantily clad strippers, burlesque girls, and prostitutes. It ceased print in 1977. Available from http://policegazette.us; accessed September 21, 2009.

5. Texarkana, Texas, is approximately ten miles north of Sulphur, Texas.

6. The Sulphur River starts in eastern Delta County, Texas, and runs eastward through Bowie and Cass counties to the Arkansas state line.

7. Jake is the English conductor the men met on the train.

8. The Capitol Hotel was built in 1881 and was named by Colonel A. Groesbeck. Available from www.hotel-online.com/News/PressReleases1998_4th/Oct98_RiceHotel.html#Rice; accessed June 15, 2009.

9. Morgan's Point, Texas, is approximately 171 miles west of Sulphur, Texas.

10. Lynchburg, Texas, is approximately 193 miles southeast of Morgan's Point, Texas.

11. A dotterel is a Eurasian form of wading bird or a plover. They are also referred to as dotes because they are regarded as slow, dim-witted, and easy to catch. They are accentuated with a broad, white eye stripe and a narrow, white band separating its breast, which is gray, from its russet-colored belly. It is about 20 centimeters (8 inches) long. It nests in tundra and in mountains across Eurasia to western Alaska and as far south as Britain and the Balkans, migrating to northern Africa and the Middle East. Available from www.britannica.com/EBchecked/topic/169791/dotterel; accessed September 17, 2011.

12. *Justine* is the name of the steamship the men are traveling on.

13. *The Mollie Mohr* was a tugboat owned by the Houston Direct Navigation Company. *The Southwestern Reporter, Volume 11* (St. Paul, MN: West Publishing Co., 1889), p. 131.

14. This book is believed to actually be "The Lives of the Queens of England," from the Norman Conquest; with Anecdotes of their Courts" (Philadelphia, PA: Blanchard and

Lea, 1868). Written by Agnes Strickland.

15. Bittern is a wading bird in the order Ciconiiformes and inhabits densely veg-
etated wetlands. The bird is in the heron family, Ardeidae, a family of wading birds.
They were called hæferblæte in Old English; the word "bittern" came to English from
Old French butor. Bitterns usually frequent reed beds and similar marshy areas, and
feed on amphibians, reptiles, insects, and fish. Forshaw, *Encyclopedia of Birds,* pp. 67,
70.

16. The American Coot bird is an all-black wading bird with a white bill and swims
similarly to a duck but does not have webbed feet. Poldoo is a reference to the Cajun
word pouldeau which means "water hen." Ted Floyd, *Smithsonian Field Guide to the Birds
of North America,* (New York: HarperCollins Publishers, 2008), p. 143.

17. Heron are wading birds from the order Ciconiiformes. They are normally white,
black, or gray and come in many sizes. Forshaw, *Encyclopedia of Birds,* p. 68.

18. Cedar Bayou, Texas, is approximately 201 miles southeast of Morgan's Point, Texas.

19. All Fours, also called seven-up or sledge, was a popular card game during the American Civil War and is considered a forebear to poker. Schwartz, *Roll the Bones: The History
of Gambling,* pp. 228, 254, 256, 279.

20. The St. Charles Hotel was a hotel in New Orleans that was a resort to wealthy plant-
ers and housed the Chamber of Commerce, the stock exchange, and numerous political
gatherings. Ludy, *Historic Hotels of the World,* pp. 254–55.

21. Oakland Park in New Orleans had just been renovated at this time and numerous
improvements had been made, like a grand amphitheatre with chairs and steam cars that
took guests to the gates and only charged five cents for the ride. "The Wild West." *New
Orleans Evening Chronicle,* December 23, 1884, page 1.

22. Captain Adam Henry Bogardus was born in Albany County New York, in 1833 and
became known as "the champion wing shot of the world." Bogardus was successful at
establishing trapshooting as a popular sport. He was a regular sharpshooter in Buffalo
Bill's Wild West show. Don Russell, *The Lives and Legends of Buffalo Bill,* (Norman, OK:
University of Oklahoma Press, 1960), p. 296.

23. William Levi "Buck" Taylor (1857–1924) was known as "The King of the Cowboys"
and a star in Buffalo Bill's show. He helped romanticize the American Cowboy with
his trick shooting, roping, and participation in staged Indian attacks. Slatta, *The Cowboy
Encyclopedia,* p. 366.

24. John Y. Nelson, also known as "Old Man Nelson," was a well-known guide, trapper,
and hunter. He guided Brigham Young across the plains to the Utah Territory in 1847
and was a scout with Buffalo Bill at Fort McPherson in 1869. He, his Sioux wife, and
their five children became a fixture of the Wild West show. Russell, *The Lives and Legends of Buffalo Bill,* p. 308.

25. The World's Industrial and Cotton Centennial Exposition was held in what is now
Audubon Park in 1884–1885. It commemorated the first shipment of cotton from the
United States in 1784 and was intended to celebrate the South's recovery from the Civil
War. The fair was a financial failure. Available from http://nutrias.org/monthly/mar99/
mar992.htm; accessed April 28, 2013.

26. The Battle of Sedan was fought September 1, 1870, during the Franco-Prussian

War. Early on September 1, Bavarian troops under General Ludwig von der Tann began crossing the Meuse and probed toward the village of Bazeilles. Entering the town, they met French troops from General Barthelemy Lebrun's XII Corps. As fighting began, the Bavarians battled the elite Infanterie de Marine, which had barricaded several streets and buildings. The French were soon overwhelmed and by midday they surrendered. Available from http://militaryhistory.about.com/od/battleswars1800s/p/Franco -Prussian-War-Battle-Of-Sedan.htm; accessed October 17, 2011.

27. Fred Archer, being a horse jockey, would normally have to maintain a weight of 112 to 114 pounds. At 133 pounds, he is overweight.

28. Keno was a popular mid-nineteenth-century lottery game in New Orleans and Mississippi. It was almost always illegal and was normally played in what was referred to as a "Keno den." Schwartz, *Roll the Bones: The History of Gambling*, pp. 376–77.

29. No information as to who Pemberton was could be found on the historical record.

30. Colonel William Fredrick "Buffalo Bill" Cody (1846–1917) was a frontiersman, scout, buffalo hunter, and entertainer. He became one of the central icons of the American Frontier. And incredibly famous when he created Buffalo Bill's Wild West Show. Richard W. Slatta, *The Cowboy Encyclopedia* (Santa Barbara, CA: ABC-CLIO, 1994), p. 72.

31. "Madame Eugenie's" is a reference to The Café Pellérin, a popular restaurant that was frequented by known actors in the area and was run by Madame Eugene until 1907. Walter Hill, "The Passing of Old New Orleans," *Uncle Remus Magazine, Volume I,* June 1907, p. 43.

32. Casekeeper used in faro refers to the man who sits across from the dealer and keeps track of each card played on an abacus-like device. Las Vegas Review-Journal, "Former Dealer Hopes for Return of Faro," available from www.reviewjournal.com/ lvrj_home/2000; accessed October 12, 2008.

33. Harlequinade first arose around 1577. It is an impromptu, slapstick comedy put on by a troupe of comedic actors. Maurice Sand, *The History of Harlequinade* (London, England: Benjamin Blom Inc., 1915), p. 37.

34. No information as to who Nick Shamville was could be found on the historical record.

35. French to English translation of Chef Menteur means "Chief Liar."

36. Lopey is most likely "Loupe," which is a common name found in New Orleans.

37. Trinity Church in New Orleans was originally constructed in 1848 by Father Masquelet at the corner of Dauphine and St. Ferdinand Streets. The church would later burn to the ground in 1851 and would be rebuilt in 1853 by Reverend Mathias Schiffer. He would serve fifteen years of service to the church before dying of yellow fever in 1866. "History of Holy Trinity Parish," available from www.neworleanschurches.com/holy trinity/holytrin.htm; accessed September 29, 2009.

38. No information as to who Mrs. Herb was could be found on the historical record.

Chapter Five: Hunting and Fishing in Florida

1. The Louisville and Nashville Railway was charted by the state of Kentucky in 1850 and operated until 1982. It operated under one name continuously for 132 years. It became one of the premier Southern Railways and extended its reach far beyond its

namesake cities, ultimately building over 7,000 miles of track. Available from http://railga.com/ln.html; accessed October 17, 2011.

2. The St. James Hotel was one of Jacksonville's grandest hotels during the tourist booms of the 1870s and 1880s. It was burnt to the ground during the Fire of 1901 when most of the city was destroyed. Available from www.jaxhistory.com/Jax%20Arch%20 Herit/D-44.htm; accessed October 17, 2011.

3. St. John's River is the longest river in the state of Florida and starts in Indian River County, Florida, and drains to the Atlantic Ocean in Duval County, Florida.

4. Tocoi, Florida, is approximately forty-two miles southwest of Jacksonville, Florida.

5. Palatka, Florida, is approximately sixty-two miles southwest of Jacksonville, Florida.

6. Sanford, Florida, is approximately ninety-two miles south of Tocoi, Florida.

7. Astatula, Florida, is approximately thirty-five miles west of Sanford, Florida.

8. Lake Monroe helps make up the St. John's River system in Florida and forms the border for Seminole and Volusia counties.

9. Rockledge, Florida, is approximately fifty-five miles southeast of Sanford, Florida.

10. Tropical House is likely a reference to the Indian River Hotel. The hotel was constructed in 1881 by A. L. Hatch and was purchased by Joseph Wilkinson in 1885. Wilkinson named it the Indian River Hotel. It was sold in 1910 to S. F. Travis. available from www.examiner.com/article/travel-into-time-at-the-indian-river-hotel-geocache-marks-the-spot; accessed April 17, 2013.

11. The Indian River in Southern Florida is an Atlantic Intracoastal Waterway and extends the border between Brevard and Voulsia counties. It is a part of the Indian River Lagoon.

12. Titusville, Florida, is approximately nineteen miles north of Rockledge, Florida.

13. Eileen is going to have puppies.

14. Raft ducks are also known as ruddy ducks. The male duck's body is a rich chestnut color and has a black and white head with a bright blue bill. The female is accentuated by a pale white cheek and no blue bill. Ted Floyd, Paul Hess, and George Scott, *Smithsonian Field Guide to the Birds of North America* (New York: HarperCollins, 2008), p. 56.

15. Oak Hill, Florida, is approximately twenty miles north of Titusville, Florida.

16. St. Sebastian River is also known as St. Sebastian Creek and shares a mouth with the Indian River Lagoon.

17. Paul Darden Parker (1866–1938) was a fisherman, boatman, and merchant in Rockledge, Florida. He lived with his wife Letitia Futch Parker. They would later move to New Smyrna, Florida. Available from "1880 United States Census," http://search.ancestry library.com/cgi-bin/sse.dll?db=1880usfedcen&h=19708461&indiv=try&o_vc=Record: OtherRecord&rhSource=6061; accessed September 28, 2011.

18. A sea eagle is also known as an erne or an ern. They vary in size and belong to the genus *Haliaeetus* in the bird of prey family Accipitridae. They are accentuated by white heads and white tail feathers. Leslie Brown and Dean Amadon, *Eagles, Hawks and Falcons of the World* (London, England: Hamlyn Publishing Group, 1968), p. 666.

19. French to English translation in this instance means the buzzards are "arriving for dinner."

20. Egrets are white plumed herons from the order Ciconiiformes. They mainly stay in

marshy wetlands. Forshaw, *Encyclopedia of Birds: A Comprehensive Illustrated Guide by International Experts,* pp. 67–68.

21. Ibis is a wetlands bird normally found in the southeast United States. Their plumage is normally white, brown, speckled, or red. They are from the genus *Eudocimus albus.* Forshaw, *Encyclopedia of Birds: A Comprehensive Illustrated Guide by International Experts,* pp. 111–12.

22. Water turkey or anhinga is a wetland bird native to the southeastern United States. It is an oversized bird with a long neck belonging to the genus *Anhinga anhinga.* Forshaw, *Encyclopedia of Birds: A Comprehensive Guide by International Experts,* p. 102.

23. This is a reference to Savannah, Georgia, and Charleston, South Carolina.

24. Fort Capron was built to replace Fort Pierce that had been destroyed by fire in 1843. Lt. Jonathan Ripley named the fort after Erastus Capron an officer in the First Artillery who showed great courage during the Second Seminole War. "Fort Capron," available from www.stluciehistoricalsociety.org/capron.html; accessed October 19, 2008.

25. Stephen Ryder (1850–) resided in Rockledge, Florida, in Brevard County he was a storekeeper and lived with his wife M. P. Ryder and their two children Florence and Stephen Jr. "1880 United States Federal Census," available from http://search.ancestry .library.com/cgi-bin/sse.dll; accessed September 21, 2009.

26. This is a reference to Miss Evelyn Bell.

27. Captain Thomas E. Richards, in 1879, established a homestead in Eden, Florida, approximately 238 miles south of Jacksonville, and planted pineapple slips on the small plantation on Hutchison Island on the mainland and near his home. All the pineapples on the mainland either died or were eaten by animals except for the ones planted near his home. By 1891, with that initial crop, Richards had the largest pineapple plantation on the Indian River in Florida. Available from www.jensen-beach-florida.com/Jensen-Beach-History.php; accessed April 30, 2009.

28. Mangrove Snapper and Red Snapper are a smaller species of fish that weigh around two to six pounds. They are very common fish in tropical regions especially in Florida. Available from www.sms.si.edu/IRLSpec/Lutjan_griseu.htm; accessed September 22, 2011.

29. A sheepshead fish normally grows ten to twenty inches in size and is accentuated by five to six dark bars on the side of its body. It is normally found from the Mid-Atlantic to Texas in the United States. Available from www.sms.si.edu/IRLSpec/Archos_probat .htm; accessed September 22, 2011.

30. The jewfish is the informal name for the Atlantic goliath grouper. These fish are normally found in tropical waters in the Bahamas, most of the Caribbean and the Florida Keys. Available from www.igfa.org/records/Fish-Records.aspx?Fish=Grouper,%20 goliath&LC=ATR; accessed September 22, 2011.

31. The Hon. Cody is believed to be a boatman or a laborer at the Florida camp. Buffalo Bill was in New Orleans at this time performing with his Wild West show.

32. Jeremiah O'Donovan Rossa (1831–1915) was an Irish freedom fighter and an advocate for Irish republicanism. In 1881 he destroyed an English military barracks killing a seven year old boy. This incident, however, is a reference to the "dynamite war" in which Irish Americans bombed the Tower of London and Houses of Parliament but did not

directly relate to Rossa. Terry Golway, *For the Cause of Liberty: A Thousand Years of Ireland's Heroes* (New York: Simon & Schuster, 2000), pp. 129–31, 178, 222.

33. Fort Pierce, Florida, is a town in St. Lucie County approximately thirteen miles north of Eden, Florida.

34. The Kennedy Rifle was developed by David Kennedy (1768–1837). He was a gunsmith in Bear Creek, North Carolina. The rifle is equipped with a brass patch box with a six-pointed star finial and a lid that does not extend all the way to the butt-plate. The weapon also features a comb that is set off from the rest of the butt-stock by a relief-carved step instead of the usual incised line. The gun was developed in 1807. Available from http://freepages.genealogy.rootsweb.ancestry.com; accessed June 2, 2009.

35. Jupiter, Florida, is approximately thirty-three miles south of Eden, Florida.

36. No information as to who Peter Wright was could be found on the historical record.

37. Henry Windsor Villers-Stuart was a British clergyman and politician. He was elected to the Waterford parliament from 1826 to 1830. Golway, *For the Cause of Liberty: A Thousand Years of Ireland's Heroes*, p. 100.

38. Lake Worth, Florida, is approximately twenty-seven miles Southeast of Jupiter, Florida.

39. "Skin" is a card game in which the lowest hand wins. It is played using a standard deck of cards, aces through kings. To begin the game each player cuts the cards to determine who will deal. The highest card deals. Each player is dealt four cards. Players look at two cards in their hand while the other two remain face down on the table (blind cards). The players rotate through four turns and must draw from the deck that has not been dealt, discard into a discard pile, and turn one card up in their hand. Available from http://wiki.answers.com/Q/How_do_you_play_Skins_Card_Game; accessed September 26, 2011.

40. "Prick the Garter" also known as "pitch the knob" is played with a "garter" or a piece of list doubled and then folded tight. The gambler then bets that he can, with a pin, prick the point where the garter is doubled. The game was notorious for cheating and was often played at a fair. John Camden Hotten, *The Slang Dictionary* or, *The Vulgar Words, Street Phrases, and Fast Expressions of High and Low Society* (London, England: John Camden Hotten, 1864), p. 260.

41. Peck's Lake, Florida, is approximately fifteen miles north of Jupiter, Florida.

42. Hope Sound, Florida, is approximately four miles south of Peck's Lake, Florida.

43. Cavalla is a reference to several different types of fish that belong to the families Carangidae and Scombridae. Available from www.britannica.com/EBchecked/topic/100545/cavalla; accessed September 26, 2011.

44. St. Lucie Inlet, Florida, is approximately six miles north of Peck Lake, Florida.

45. This is a reference to Petersburg, Virginia. It was the second largest city in Virginia at the time and was a very strategic point during the Civil War.

46. This is a reference to the book *Memoirs of William T. Sherman*, by himself (New York: D. Appleton & Company, 1875).

47. The siege of Khartoum lasted from March 12, 1884, to January 26, 1885, in Sudan. A combined army of British and Egyptians led by Major-General Charles Gordon fought against Mahdist Sudanese troops and would eventually be massacred in an attempt to

evacuate the city and Sudan. Denis Judd, *Empire: The British Imperial Experience from 1765 to the Present* (New York: HarperCollins Publishers, 1996), pp. 99–100.

48. Raymond Rodgers Belmont (1863–1887) was the son of famous American politician and former chairman of the Democratic National Committee August Belmont. Raymond would ride horses with Evelyn Booth and Dr. J. P. Frizzle in Buffalo Bill's Wild West Show while in New Orleans. He died only a few years later at the age of twenty-three. Available from http://trees.ancestrylibrary.com/tree/46572238/person /6563528764; accessed September 15, 2014, and *New Orleans Times-Democrat*." Millionare Cowboys," March 31, 1885, page 4. Accessed October 2, 2012.

49. No information as to who Mygatt was could be found on the historical record.

50. The SS *America* was built in 1863. The boat traveled between Cuba and Boston, Massachusetts, on a regular basis. In 1885, the boat encountered a winter gale off the coast of Florida that caused leaks in the vessel's hull. Captain F. C. Miller decided to run the vessel ashore near Stuart, Florida. The crew was able to escape before the boat was torn to pieces. Michael C. Barnette, *Encyclopedia of Florida Shipwrecks, Volume I: Atlantic Coast*, (Florida: The Association of Underwater Explorers, 2010) pp. 14-15.

51. Colson was first mate on the steamship *America*. Barnette, *Encyclopedia of Florida Shipwrecks, Volume I: Atlantic Coast*, (Florida: The Association of Underwater Explorers, 2010) pp. 14-15.

52. This is an Irish slang phrase that relates to "taking the biscuit" or "Abernethy Biscuit" and means to be regarded (by the speaker) as a most surprising thing that could have occurred. Available from www.thefreedictionary.com/biscuit; accessed September 27, 2011.

53. Fort Pierce, Florida, is approximately thirteen miles north of Eden, Florida.

54. New Haven is most likely a reference to Melbourne, Florida, that is approximately twenty-five miles south of Rockledge, Florida.

55. Clarence M. Bevan (1850–1917) was a resident of Saint Johns, Florida. He was married to Florence Hulett, and his occupation was noted as a "Gentleman of Leisure" and as a "Capitalist." Available from http://search.ancestrylibrary.com/cgi-bin/sse.dll?new=1 &gsfn=Clarence&gsln=Bevan&rank=1&gss=angs-g&mswpn__ftp=Florida%2c+USA& mswpn=12&mswpn_PInfo=5-%7c0%7c1652393%7c0%7c2%7c3245%7c12%7c0%7c0% 7c0%7c0%7c&msbdy=1850&pcat=ROOT_CATEGORY&h=6007946&db=1880usfed cen&indiv=1&ml_rpos=2; accessed September 15, 2014.

56. St. Augustine, Florida, is approximately 120 miles north of Rockledge, Florida.

57. Merritt Island, Florida, is approximately 101 miles north of Eden, Florida.

58. New Smyrna is approximately twelve miles south of Daytona Beach, Florida.

59. The Magruders lived in Brevard and Rockledge, Florida. The family consisted of Cephus Baily Magruder (1828–1910) who was a horticulturist and father. He is referred to by Booth as "Old Man Magruder." He lived with his wife Cornelia and seven children: Charles, George, Jamie, Albert, Sarah, Hubert, and Lawson. He is said to have named the town Rockledge in 1876 because of where he built his home. "1880 United States Federal Census," available from http://search.ancestry.library.com/cgi-bin/sse.dll; accessed September 21, 2011.

60. "Budd" Wilkinson is a reference to Joseph Wilkinson who bought, and named, the

Indian River Hotel in 1885. Available from www.examiner.com/article/travel-into
-time-at-the-indian-river-hotel-geocache-marks-the-spot; accessed April 17, 2013.
61. Robert C. May (1842–1918) was a private in the Confederate Army during the civil
war and served in the Jefferson Davis Legion, Mississippi Cavalry Regiment. He is listed
in the 1885 Florida State census as a fruit grower and is the father of three children:
Wellie, J Houston, and Mary M May. Available from http://search.ancestrylibrary.com/
cgi-bin/sse.dll?rank=1&new=1&MSAV=1&msT=1&gss=angs-g&gsfn=Charles&gsln=
May&msbdy=1840&msrpn__ftp=Rockledge%2c+Brevard%2c+Florida%2c+USA&msr
pn=16117&msrpn_PInfo=8-|0|1652393|0|2|3245|12|0|370|16117|0|&catBucket=rstp
&uidh=x14&=b%2cr%2c0&_83004003-n_xcl=f&pcat=ROOT_CATEGORY&h=1070
3&recoff=2+3&db=FloridaStateCen1867&indiv=1; accessed September 28, 2011.
62. Stuart's Calvary is a reference to James Ewell Brown (J.E.B.) Stuart's Calvary.
63. The Mahdist War that waged from 1881–1889 was led by the Mahdi, an inspira-
tional religious leader, who rose to power in Egypt in 1881. The Mahdi rallied pious
tribesmen of the Sudan around him and many Egyptian provinces fell under his control.
After the slaughter of Colonel William Hicks and the disastrous Siege of Khartoum
the British abandoned the Sudan in 1886. But a decade later in 1896 the British would
return and invade the Sudan. Judd, *Empire: The British Imperial Experience from 1765 to
the Present*, pp. 99–100.

Chapter Six: Shootout with Bill and the Journey Home
1. Animalcules is the name given to micro-organisms that Dutch natural history stu-
dent Antony van Leeuwenhoek discovered while looking at many different types of
materials in over 247 microscopes at varying levels of magnification. Available from
http://dimdima.com/science/science_common/show_science.asp?q_aid=88&q_
title=Animalcules+Discovered; accessed October 22, 2011.
2. This is most likely a reference to the steamship *Waunita*. This steamship was built in
Jacksonville, Florida, in 1882. The boat was seventy-seven feet long with a twenty-two-
foot beam. The owner of the boat was Captain John Smith. His boating business was
established in 1860 and was incorporated in 1888. It was part of the Rockledge Florida
Steamboat line. Available from www.floridamemory.com/items/show/149057; accessed
September 15, 2014.
3. Edward de Courey (1850-) was born in New York, New York, and lived in Providence,
Rhode Island, for a period of time before moving to Florida. Available from http://
search.ancestrylibrary.com/cgi-bin/sse.dll?new=1&gsfn=Edward&gsln=De+Courey&ra
nk=1&gss=angs-g&mswpn__ftp=New+York%2c+USA&mswpn=35&mswpn_PInfo=5-
%7c0%7c1652393%7c0%7c2%7c3244%7c35%7c0%7c0%7c0%7c0%7c&msbdy=1850&
pcat=ROOT_CATEGORY&h=351611&db=RICensus&indiv=1&ml_rpos=1; accessed
September 16, 2014.
4. Georgiana, Florida, is approximately seven miles southeast of Rockledge, Florida.
5. Lucius Littauer (1859–1944) eventually became an American politician, businessman,
and college football coach. He served in the United States House of Representatives for
five terms from 1897 to 1907. He helped to found Harvard's Graduate School of Educa-
tion that eventually became the John F. Kennedy School of Government. Available from

www.hks.harvard.edu/about/history; accessed September 13, 2014.

6. Mrs. Richards is a reference to Rebecca J. Richards (1833–) who was married to Captain Thomas E. Richards the pineapple farmer who was previously identified in Chapter Five. Available from http://search.ancestrylibrary.com/iexec?htx=View&r=55 42&dbid=7602&iid=004120037_00418&fn=Thomas+E&ln=Richards&st=r&ssrc=& pid=33979635; accessed October 22, 2011.

7. No information as to who "Old Man Wilder" was could be found on the historical record.

8. Enterprise, Florida, is approximately sixty-three miles northwest of Rockledge, Florida.

9. The steamship *Anita* was owned by the Clyde Steamship company and shipped from New York City to Charleston to points on the St. Johns River in Florida. In 1889, the ship was deemed worthless and was burned in Boston, Massachusetts, in the summer of that year. *The Southern Reporter, Volume 19: Containing all the Decisions of the Supreme Courts of Alabama, Louisiana, Florida, Mississippi Permanent Edition March 4, 1896 – June17, 1896* (St. Paul, Minn.: West Publishing Company, 1896), p. 641.

10. Beaver Street is located in Jacksonville, Florida.

11. Frank B. "Yank" Adams (1847–1923) was a famous finger billiardist from Chicago. He was known to not play with a cue and did marvelous displays of tricks and difficult shots with his fingers. He was largely self-taught from an early age. He was often dubbed as the "Digital Billiard Wonder" and would shoot the balls by twisting the ball between his thumb and middle finger. He often played to a crowd of a thousand spectators in a small venue. He has been called the greatest billiards exhibition player that ever lived. "Famous Finger Billiardist Turns Up In New York." *The Salt Lake Tribune*, February 10, 1923, page 12.

12. Charles Martin Bixamos was a former prize fighter from Washington County, Mississippi. He was defeated via decision by Jack "Nonpareil" Dempsey in March 1885 (some records report March 14, 1885). Fleischer, *The Ring Boxing Encyclopedia and Record Book*, p. 138.

13. George Fryer was a former prize fighter who would later fight for the middleweight championship of the east against Billy Leedom. The fight with Leedom would be stopped before its completion by special guest referee, Arthur Chambers. Available from www.cyberboxingzone.com/boxing/leedom-billy.htm; accessed April 8, 2009.

14. Charles Lange was a former prize fighter who fought George Fryer in 1885. Jack "Nonpareil" Dempsey was the guest referee for that bout. Lange would be knocked out in eleven rounds. "Charles Lange," available from www.cyberboxingzone.com/boxing/non-jack.htm; accessed April 8, 2009.

15. The Grand Opera House was a well-known and formal establishment that was seen as a type of resort. It showcased everything from theater to live bands. One of the famous bands that played in this time period was "The Razzy Dazzy Spasm Band." Asbury, *The French Quarter: An Informal History of the New Orleans Underworld*, p. 438.

16. Molly Johnson, whose real name was Mary Buckley, was from St. Louis but settled in Louisiana. She was a prostitute for the famed Madame Kate Townsend. After Townsend's violent death at the hands of Treville Sykes in 1883, Molly took over

Townsend's brothel and ran it until her death in 1889. After her death, the contents of the brothel were sold at public auction and the brothel was then closed. Asbury, *The French Quarter: An Informal History of the New Orleans Underworld,* pp. 373–74, 377.

17. The "Cowboys" are Buffalo Bill's Wild West Cowboys.

18. There is no account of a Miss B left on any historical record.

19. "Con" T. Groner, also known as Con "Grover," was born in Columbia County, Ohio, where he fought during the Civil War as part of the Company D 72nd Ohio Regiment. He was injured seven times during his time in the military. From there, he moved west where he became a fireman engineer for the Union Pacific Railroad. He would later become one of Buffalo Bill's Wild West Cowboys and was often referred to as the "Cowboy Sheriff of the Platte." "The William F. Cody Archive: Documenting the Life and Times of an American icon," available from http://codyarchive.org/memorabilia/wfc.prog.1884.html; accessed February 11, 2014.

20. A match was shot at New Orleans, March 28, between W. F. Cody (Buffalo Bill) and Evelyn Booth, with fifty clay pigeons, the latter winning by a score of 40 to 39. April 1, the same gentlemen had another match, Mr. Cody winning by a score of 47 to 46. "Our Monthly Record," *The Outing, Volume 6* (Boston: The Wheelman Company, 1885), p. 378.

21. Major John Burke was the general manager and press agent for Buffalo Bill's Wild West show. He had worked with Cody since 1872 when Bill was an actor. "How the Wild West Show Has Developed; The First Performance Was on the Fourth of July, 1881. Col. Cody's Success in Europe – How Our Cowboys Proved Their Prowess – Major Burke's Reminiscences." *New York Times,* page 26, April 7, 1901.

22. This is a reference to Black Hills, South Dakota.

23. This is a reference to Buffalo Bill's ranch in North Platte, Nebraska.

24. Frascati Park was located on Bay Shore Road in Mobile, Alabama. J. Boardman, *Acts of the General Assembly of the State of Alabama* (Alabama, J. Boardman, 1889), p. 1068.

25. Pearl and Queenie are most likely prostitutes who work for Miss Emma Johnson who was a prominent prostitute at the time and would later become a well-known madam, around 1900, for the House of all Nations that was a notorious sex circus that operated on Basin Street in New Orleans. Long, *Great Southern Babylon: Sex, Race, and Respectability in New Orleans 1865–1920,* p. 142.

26. Captain Hyatt refers to Henry J. Hyatt (1858–) who worked for the New Orleans Police Force. He married Annie Gottschalk in 1892. He is listed as a police sergeant but could perhaps have been calling himself a captain. Available from http://search.ancestrylibrary.com/cgi-bin/sse.dll?new=1&gsfn=Henry&gsln=Hyatt&rank=1&gss=angs-g&mswpn__ftp=New+Orleans%2c+Orleans%2c+Louisiana%2c+USA&mswpn=34322&mswpn_PInfo=8-%7c0%7c1652393%7c0%7c2%7c3246%7c21%7c0%7c2249%7c34322%7c0%7c&msbdy=1858&pcat=ROOT_CATEGORY&h=9713689&db=1910USCenIndex&indiv=1&ml_rpos=3; accessed September 19, 2014.

27. This is most likely a reference to Arta Cody (1866–1904). She was Buffalo Bill's first daughter from Louisa Frederici of St. Louis. Available from www.findagrave.com/cgi-bin/fg.cgi?page=gr&GRid=2887; accessed October 3, 2011.

28. This is a reference to Buffalo Bill's acting career, which started in 1872. He acted in

infamous dime novelist Ned Buntline's play called *The Scouts of the Prairie*, which was also known as *Red Deviltry* as It Is. Slatta, *The Cowboy Encyclopedia*, p. 55.

29. The steamship *Bernard Hall* was built in England in 1880. The ship was 338 feet long, had a 38-foot beam, and was 26-feet deep. The vessel weighed 2,678 tons and belonged to the West India and Pacific Steamship Company Limited, of Liverpool, England. "Article 3—No Title," *New York Times*, August 16 1901. Accessed April 17, 2013. http://query.nytimes.com/mem/archive-free/pdf?res=FB0F12F83F5B11738DDD AF0994D0405B818CF1D3.

30. The Floridian was built in 1884 and was later sold to Fredrick Leyland and Company in 1900. The ship was scrapped eight years later in 1908. Available from www .theshipslist.com/ships/lines/wip.shtml; accessed June 1, 2013.

31. No information as to who Mrs. Purnell was could be found on the historical record.

32. This is probably a reference to Harry H. Freedman who was a women's baseball promoter in the 1880s. He was accused of recruiting women for his baseball teams to serve as prostitutes. While his "buxom beauties" were playing in New Orleans, he was accused by several parents of trying to entice their daughters to join his baseball club. Cora was most likely enticed by Freedman. Gai Ingham Berlage, *Women in Baseball: The Forgotten History* (Westport, CT: Greenwood Publishing Group, Inc., 1994), p. 28.

33. Pat Duffy was a local New Orleans gambler and boxing promoter. He promoted a fight between John L. Sullivan and Jake Kilrain, a battle that was eventually won by Sullivan via TKO in seventy-five rounds. Duffy was also a business partner of Bud Renaud, promoter and gambler, and the two amassed a small fortune promoting several fights that attendees did not know where or when the fights would take place until the day of the event. Isenberg, *John L. Sullivan and His America*, pp. 266–75.

34. Gonorrheal ophthalmia produces an acute purulent conjunctivitis that appears two to five days after birth or earlier with premature rupture membranes. The neonate has severe eyelid edema followed by chemosis and a profuse purulent exudates that may be under pressure. If untreated, corneal ulcerations and blindness may occur.

35. In the 1870s, Canal Street was home to Moreau's Restaurant, between St. Charles and Carondelet streets. In its day it was considered the best restaurant in New Orleans. By the twentieth century, Moreau's was gone. Peggy Scott Laborde and John Magill, *Canal Street: New Orleans Great Wide Way* (Gretna, LA: Pelican Publishing Company, 2006), p. 17.

36. Judge Walker is a reference to James Campbell Walker (1840–1900). He was a lawyer in 1880 and later became a judge. He was married to Corine Walker. They had three children: Katie, James, and Livingston. Available from http://search.ancestrylibrary.com/ cgi-bin/sse.dll?new=1&gsfn=James&gsln=Walker&rank=1&gss=angs-g&mswpn__ftp =New+Orleans%2c+Orleans%2c+Louisiana%2c+USA&mswpn=34322&mswpn_ PInfo=8-%7c0%7c1652393%7c0%7c2%7c3246%7c21%7c0%7c2249%7c34322%7c0%7 c&msbdy=1840&pcat=ROOT_CATEGORY&h=40210354&db=1880usfedcen&indiv =1&ml_rpos=1; accessed September 23, 2014.

37. Bidwell is most likely a reference to John Bidwell (1819–1900). He was an American pioneer who struck it rich in the California Gold Rush. He was also a farmer, soldier in the Mexican-American War, member of the Bear Flag revolt, statesman, politician,

prohibitionist, and philanthropist. He founded an emigrant party known as the Bartelson-Bidwell Party and is also the founder of the town of Chico, California. In 1875, he ran for governor of California on the Anti-Monopoly ticket. He became most well known for his activism in the temperance movement and presided over the Prohibition Party. In 1880, he was the Prohibition candidate for governor and in 1888 ran for office of president on the Prohibition ticket. Michael J. Gillis and Michael F. Magliari, *John Bidwell and California: The Life and Writings of a Pioneer 1841–1900*, (Spokane, WA: Arthur H. Clark Company, 2003), p. 19.

38. Samuel Plimsoll (1824–1898) brought about one of the greatest shipping revolutions ever known by shocking the British nation into making reforms that have saved the lives of countless men. Plimsoll took up, as a crusade, the plan of James Hall to require that vessels bear a load line marking and indicating when they were overloaded, hence ensuring the safety of crew and cargo. In 1876, Plimsoll forced Parliament to pass the Unseaworthy Ships Bill into law requiring that vessels to bear the load line freeboard marking. It was soon known as the "Plimsoll Mark" and was eventually adopted by all maritime nations of the world. He visited the United States to try and secure less bitter tone against the British, which was being taught in American classrooms. William Kirkwood Purves, David Sadava, Gordon H. Orians, and H. Craig Heller, *Life, the Science of Biology* (New York: Macmillan, 2004), p. 1104.

39. Ellen Plimsoll (1867–) was the adopted daughter of Samuel and Eliza Plimsoll. Available from http://search.ancestrylibrary.com/cgi-bin/sse.dll?rank=1&new=1&MSAV=0&msT=1&gss=angs-g&gsfn=Ellen&gsln=Plimsoll&uidh=x14&=y%2c0&pcat=ROOT_CATEGORY&h=14059126&db=uki1871&indiv=1; accessed October 22, 2011.

40. "Waggle" is a reference to one of the hunting dogs Booth had with him.

41. Ellen and Button are the names of two hunting dogs that Booth had with him.